W9-BNV-868

# THE JESUS COMMUNITY

## A THEOLOGY OF RELATIONAL FAITH

# Rubel Shelly
# &John O. York

LEAFWOOD
PUBLISHERS

THE JESUS COMMUNITY
*A Theology of Relational Faith*
published by Leafwood Publishers

Copyright © 2004 by Rubel Shelly & John O. York

ISBN 0-9748441-3-6
Printed in the United States of America

*Cover design by Rick Gibson*

ALL RIGHTS RESERVED
No part of this publication may be reproduced, stored in a retrieval system, or transmitted in any form by any means—electronic, mechanical, photocopying, recording or otherwise—without prior written consent.

For information:
Leafwood Publishers, Siloam Springs, AR
1-877-634-6004 (toll free)

Visit our website: www.leafwoodpublishers.com

04  05  06  07  08  09      9  8  7  6  5  4  3  2  1

*To our wives,*

*Myra & Anne,*

*who continue to show us*

*the authentic & transforming nature*

*of the Jesus community.*

# TABLE OF CONTENTS

# PREFACE

One sometimes hears the question nowadays: *Can the church survive?* Such a question is absurd, even heretical, if we are talking about the kingdom people for whom Christ died, called out of the world, and called into community as a Living Temple for the Holy Spirit. The promise of Jesus that nothing—not even the dreadful powers of the unseen world— would prevail against the church makes the question nonsensical for all who confess Christ as Lord and Savior. Even centuries of doctrinal debate and division among Christ's followers cannot derail the promises of Christ himself to be "the Way, the Truth, and the Life."

The church that will survive both the onslaught of Satan and the ineptitude of Christians is secure by divine decree. But *that* church is sometimes nothing more than an abstraction to struggling disciples and seeking unbelievers. We need specific and locatable groups of people to whom we can point those in search of spiritual formation. We need nurturing communities in which the life of Jesus is enfleshed daily—not simply discussed on Sundays—through worship, personal encouragement in faith, loving restoration in times of failure, and sustained hope by the power of the Holy Spirit. We need second-incarnation outposts of Christ's disciples around the world who make his presence felt.

Scripture is clear on this point: God's redemptive activity comes into focus in Christ and in his promise to sustain the kingdom people he has called to himself. From the church's inception on the first Pentecost Sunday following the death and resurrection and ascension of Jesus, "those being saved" are always saved in the context of community. The salvation of individuals in the biblical narrative is always simultaneously a community experience. Thus every person who experiences redemption, renewal, and transformation in Christ is also added to the church. Which church? Christ's. His one body composed of all those in every age who have been born from above. When Paul said that "God's firm foundation stands, bearing this inscription: 'The Lord knows those who are his'" (2 Tim. 2:19), it was this one church that exists across all ages that he had in mind. It is the safe repository in which all who come to Christ for salvation are sheltered until he returns to claim those who belong to him.

Very few of us, however, live with this abstract definition of "church" in mind. History, culture, doctrinal debate and division, lists of denominations, and highway signs combine to make us think of church in practical terms of Catholic and Protestant, Presbyterian and Baptist, yours and mine. So when most of us use the term "church" we are not thinking in terms of careful New Testament definitions but historically conditioned experiences.

Thinking in those cultural and experiential terms in the mid-twentieth century, the claim "There is no salvation outside the church" was a judgment. Uttered by a Roman Catholic, it meant that Protestants were unfaithful, wrong, and/or lost—and vice versa when uttered by a Protestant. When spoken by someone from a particular Protestant denomination to someone of a different denomination, it was sometimes a similar judgment that the person who was not a member of *my* (historically conditioned) church was going to hell or a challenge to debate the relative orthodoxy of your apostate denomination versus my true, authentic, orthodox, and pleasing-to-God (culturally conditioned) church. In the early twenty-first century, many Christians are willing to recognize those perspectives as both arrogant and false. But there are other cultural definitions that also mislead us. Today's widely held cynical views about church often lead to the conclusion that most churches are hypocritical at best, and otherwise a burden to bear in the name of our salvation. This historically conditioned entity identified as church in our time has typically followed one of two business (i.e., institutional) models. One is the *corporation model* with headquarters and branch offices spread around the country or world. The corporate headquarters may be the original "mother" church or denominational headquarters. There may be great variety among the branches, much like General Motors manufactures different brands of automobiles. But the final decisions come from the top.

> *Locality, nationality, particularity are essential marks of the universal Church; the local congregation is the embodiment at a given place and time of the Church of all the world.*
>
> —Alan Richardson

The other is the *franchise model* in which each church is independently owned and operated, but there is a shared, uniform identity. Thus, even when one goes from one franchise location to the next, the same manual of instruction produces uniformity of practice. In some cases it may be the historic creeds that provide that franchise identity. In other cases it may be less-obvious oral law that maintains the framework. In the latter case, uniformity of thought and practice is a high priority because identity typically rests in the unique franchise practices. Much like restaurant chains, if a particular franchise changes the recipes, it can hardly be identified any longer as a legitimate member of the franchise.

We hope it is obvious that the corporate headquarters model and the franchise model of church both contribute to the cynicism that jeopardizes the desire to be part of a local church—even when one longs to be joined to Christ. While these understandings have functioned to separate and distinguish the various tribal identities within Christendom, they seldom have drawn Christ's kingdom people closer to one another. Worse still, those seeking meaningful spiritual identity too often experience Christianity only as a system of beliefs being debated by entrenched devotees.

On the one hand, there is comfort in knowing that God is greater than all these institutional models of church. Yes, God alone knows our hearts, so God alone ultimately knows who belongs to him. And, yes, there are likely more than a few people in the past couple of millennia who have claimed church membership for social, economic, or political gain but who never actually experienced Christ as Savior in any meaningful way. Similarly, it also seems altogether likely that there are people who have obeyed the rules for joining and maintaining fellowship with the institutional church but who have never even entertained the thought that their right-standing with the institutional church is ultimately neither a guarantee of membership in the one church of which Scripture speaks nor a means to an authentic, life-transforming relationship with Jesus Christ.

An assumption of both the historically conditioned church and the contemporary corporation and franchise models for church is reflected in our very use of the term "institutional church" in the preceding paragraph. The first-century church was—by common and universal agreement—a single church and not a hodgepodge of denominations. To ask "What denomination do you belong to?" or "Where do you go to church?" makes perfectly good sense to us but would mystify James or Priscilla or Titus.

Instead of multiple denominations in a city, the New Testament speaks of the church at Jerusalem or the church of God at Corinth. Those whole-city churches met and functioned principally as a loose network of house churches. They were organic and relational, and the typical small-scale assembly of a house church would have been quite spontaneous and participatory in nature. Since then culture has so impinged upon church that it has become far more organized and institutional, and the typical assembly of the large-scale church is programmed by leaders, passive for spectators, and easy to "attend" without ever forming a sense of community with others who show up.

It is in this cultural context that we can understand the concern many have for the survival—or, perhaps, viability—of the church in the twenty first century. We have now lived through a full generation of American culture and church practice in which the growing conviction among many has been "Jesus, yes; church, no." We now live in a world tired of debate, wearied of Christianity and church as a system of beliefs to be argued rather than a shared life to be lived. We sense burnout with bureaucratic, program-driven, and impersonal churches and hear the cry for a genuine priesthood of believers in communities where the Spirit of God can empower one-another ministry of the most personal and practical sort.

It was this sense of longing for church as a life to be lived, empowered by God's Spirit, that led us to preach and then write *The Jesus Proposal*.[1] In that work we sought to turn attention away from all of the hair-splitting, dogma-centered readings of our past and return again to the core of faith—Jesus. We talked at length about relational faith, about our being joined to the death, resurrection, and exaltation of Jesus, and about the invitation into intimate relationship with God and one another through faith in his redeeming act of love. We talked about living in a new world in which once more we could embrace the presence of the Holy Spirit as a real presence in our lives. The next imperative is to think through and implement a form of church life that releases Christ's disciples from institutional intimidation and emboldens us for body life under our one head. We must learn how to implement family life in our Father's house.

*The Jesus Proposal* primarily addressed a means by which Christians could stop arguing with one another and share a foundational focus on Jesus as the giver and leader of our shared spiritual journeys. Only at the most general of levels did we begin to address relational faith lived in the context of church/body-of-Christ life. It is this latter task that we wish to address in this book.[2] What does a *Jesus Proposal* church look like? How can the historically conditioned, culturally experienced entity we have come to call church live out her kingdom calling as a community empowered by the Spirit to demonstrate relational faith? How can we close the distance between our idealized vision of the Kingdom or God's universal church and our sometimes-disappointing particular experiences of church in our time?

> *Now you are the body of Christ and individually members of it.*
>
> —1 Corinthians 12:27

While many disciples have begun to live in the joy of whole-person faith and salvation, we now need to start living out relational faith as particular churches. The old wineskin of brittle institutional churches simply cannot contain the fresh, Spirit-given wine of relational faith. So what does it mean for communities to bear witness to the living Christ—to each other and to the world? How do we move beyond the motives and motivations of corporate business vision statements to authentic witness that bears salvation to those who have not yet experienced Christ? How do we break through the generational and worldview barriers that seem to be bringing not healing but more divisive spirits to God's church?

It is our conviction that Christians always (and only) experience the embodied Christ or universal church in particular settings. Rather than particular churches being a branch office or a franchise, *each church is a microcosm of the whole*. One experiences the church universal in the setting of a community of people embodying Christ to one another and to their social-cultural matrix. In such distinct settings, both Christians and churches are known by their fruit. Thus the effectiveness of the bride of Christ in bearing witness to her bridegroom depends on a strategy of beauty and joy among Christians. Peter counseled the wives of unbelieving men to be such spiritually beautiful women that "even if some of them do not obey the word, they may be won over without a word by their wives' conduct, when they see the purity and reverence of your lives" (1 Pet. 3:1-2). We believe this is the way for the church today to win people to the Savior.

A lost world is not terribly likely to listen to a total stranger tell its citizens they are sinners on the way to hell whose only hope is to be found in Jesus Christ. It is altogether possible, however, that it will listen to a humble, gentle church that builds bridges of friendship, love, and service with it. They will be captivated by a love that requires God's own love to explain it—and won over through the same lifestyle that enabled Jesus to make the kingdom of God desirable to people who were utterly turned off to institutional, clergy-dominated, edifice-centered, and impersonal religion in his own time. Read the simple Gospel stories again. See how comfortable people were with him. See how naturally they were drawn to his message about a Loving Father. He was neither obsessive nor obtrusive nor obnoxious. When we imitate him and avoid the pitfalls of religiosity, we will be his body—not in caricature but in reality.

In the first-century church, among those first imitators of Christ, Satan was still at work trying to derail the Christ-experiences and efforts of Christians—even though the war already had been won at the cross. We do not want to underestimate the powers of evil in our world even now to derail a singular focus on Jesus. While we believe that this so-called Postmodern Age has marvelous opportunities for the church to be Christ to our world, there is the potential for even more division and destruction in the name of "saving the church." God's kingdom doesn't need yet another claim by us or anyone else that there is a new "formula" for church, a new method to fix all of the wrong-headed people around us. We pray this work will not be received with any such expectation or claim. It is certainly not offered with any such spirit. We simply propose a series of ideas that we believe are true to the heart of God and the teachings of Scripture. To the degree to which they serve to point us all toward more intimate relationships in the body of Christ and deeply experienced lives of worship, we give God the glory and praise.

We pray for body to honor head and for each member to be unified with every other in him. We pray for the tyranny of pressing our human opinions and best interpretations on doctrinal tangents to give way to the proclamation of the core message of the gospel. We pray for an experience of the church as the corporate expression of Christ's presence in the world and the abandonment of church as a religious corporation. We pray to experience the righteousness, joy, and peace of the community of Jesus in this world. In a word, we pray, *Our Lord, come!*

Rubel Shelly
John O. York

## Notes

1. Rubel Shelly and John O. York, *The Jesus Proposal: A Theological Framework for Maintaining the Unity of the Body of Christ* (Siloam Springs, AR: Leafwood Publishers, 2003). If you have picked up this book but do not have the background of reading the earlier one, we strongly suggest that you hold off reading it until you have worked through *The Jesus Proposal.*

2. Our title *The Jesus Community* is intended to parallel *The Jesus Proposal.* We even considered subtitling this book something like "Putting *The Jesus Proposal* into Practice" or "Living out *The Jesus Proposal.*" This book attempts to answer the question that has been put to us repeatedly by people who have been positive in their reaction to the former one: How does this proposal play out in practical terms for a local church?

*The greatest proof of
God's love is a life
that needs his love
to explain it.*

—Anonymous


*God's fingers can touch
nothing but to mold
it into loveliness.*

—George MacDonald

# 1. WHY "CHURCH" IS A DIRTY WORD FOR SO MANY

*Then I bathed you with water and washed off the blood from you, and anointed you with oil. I clothed you with embroidered cloth and with sandals of fine leather; I bound you in fine linen and covered you with rich fabric. I adorned you with ornaments: I put bracelets on your arms, a chain on your neck, a ring on your nose, earrings in your ears, and a beautiful crown upon your head. You were adorned with gold and silver, while your clothing was of fine linen, rich fabric, and embroidered cloth. You had choice flour and honey and oil for food. You grew exceedingly beautiful, fit to be a queen. Your fame spread among the nations on account of your beauty, for it was perfect because of my splendor that I had bestowed on you, says the Lord GOD.*
                                                    —Ezekiel 16:9-14

B eauty fit for a queen! Yahweh conferred it upon his covenant-bride, Israel. And the point of that beauty was that the Lord could offer Israel "as a light to the nations, that my salvation may reach to the end of the earth" (Isa. 49:6). Beauty would be central to the strategy of turning heads and capturing hearts. Charm and grace would cause others to join the joyous dance as a holy nation moved to the music of heaven. The kingdoms of earth would give way to the righteous, joyous, and peaceful Kingdom of God.

As we shall point out directly, that simple strategy failed because Israel could not be saved from the abuse of its status as a chosen people. A beautiful bride was disloyal to the One who had loved her, rescued her, and beautified her. So it was only natural that a New Testament writer like Paul—who was steeped in Jewish literature and thought—would transfer such appealing imagery to the church. In a text often expounded as a commentary on marital responsibilities, Paul is in fact more interested in using the bride-groom relationship to communicate insights about the church. "This is a great mystery, and I am applying it to Christ and the church" (Eph. 5:32)

The church is the redeemed people of God from many races, colors, and tongues who have been made one in Christ. It is the total body of those who have been called out of the world and into Christ. Or, under the metaphor that goes all the way back to Israel as Yahweh's fit-to-be-a-queen bride, the church is Christ's bride.

Husbands, love your wives, just as Christ loved the church and gave himself up for her, in order to make her holy by cleansing her with the washing of water by the word, so as to present the church to himself in splendor, without a spot or wrinkle or anything of the kind—yes, so that she may be holy and without blemish (Eph. 5:25-28).

She is to move with grace and charm to bear the aroma of Christ throughout the world. She is supposed to preserve her purity, deal gently with her admirers, come alongside the distressed with humility, and turn hearts to her Beloved. It is the ancient strategy of beauty as a light on a hill—drawing weary and dispirited pilgrims to safety. That is the *plan,* but it can hardly be said to be the lived reality of the church in today's world.

## Disappointment With the Church

The very term "church" is a dirty word to many people. And what a pity that is, since Christ Jesus intends for the church to bear witness to him throughout the world. For these unreceptive souls, however, church has been the address for a vindictive God, his abusive shepherds, and a joyless flock. They have been taught that God's love is conditioned either on irrational submission (i.e., blind obedience to human leaders) or gift exchange (i.e., money); they have read headlines about priests who are pedophiles and sexual abusers, watched the TV shenanigans of big-haired and oily-tongued hucksters who were using Jesus' name to fleece their video flocks, and heard about priests, preachers, and pew-packers frequenting adult bookstores and massage parlors.

They have listened to the Pollyanna testimonies of Christians for whom faith means that everything is always hunky-dory—only to watch them crash and burn when they lost their business, got cancer, or had a daughter get pregnant at thirteen. They have been regaled over and over again by these very same people with the Four Spiritual Laws or the Five Steps to Salvation as their only hope of escaping hell if they should die tonight. "What if the hypocrites, snake-oil salespeople, and failed-faith witnesses to Jesus as 'my personal Savior' were the ones to die tonight?" they say to themselves. "Mightn't the world be a happier, friendlier place without them?"

Onlookers who had heard of the Groom went looking to find him through the "beauty of holiness" (1 Chron. 16:29b KJV) with which it was reported the Bride was robed. They looked for the brilliance of her purity, the dignity of her devotion. They expected to be captivated by her preoccupation with—even her very worship of—her dear companion. With a certain degree of selfishness, they even expected to share in his reputed generosity through her outstretched hand. But far too many have experienced her as cold, hard, self-absorbed, and miserly. So they have been disappointed. They have turned away. Failing to see beauty, they speak instead of her lack of appeal—even of her repulsiveness.

And we wonder why so many in our world are turned off to Christianity! We wonder why they are so hostile to the idea of prayer in public schools or faith-based initiatives that will get some of their tax dollars? "Well, they're just ungodly souls who won't hear the truth!" someone says. That may be true of some, but many of these people are the most ethically sensitive and professionally upright, family-dedicated and community-involved people you will ever meet.

These people will not hear Christ's message of salvation favorably until its bearer (i.e., the church) is saved first! And the church *does* need saving from itself—its hypocrisies, injustices, and authoritarianism. The church must get outside itself—or perhaps, better, it must get over itself—in order to belie the image of an us-versus-them attitude of superiority and judgment. To be credible, it must become much less institutional and far more relational, less defensive of itself and its history and more confessional of its insufficiencies and failures, far less materialistic and self-serving and more generous and loving toward people, movements, and entities it cannot control or manipulate. In order to be convincing to people who didn't grow up inside it and learn how to turn blind eyes to its obvious defects, the church must get over its addiction to religious power and learn the healthy lifestyle of spiritual vulnerability.

> *Organized Christianity has probably done more to retard the ideals that were its founder's than any other agency in the world.*
>
> —Richard Le Gallienne

A recent book that develops the commonly heard thesis that "more wars have been waged, more people killed, and these days more evil perpetuated in the name of religion than by any other institutional force in human history" grants that the topic of religion evokes a wide range of responses. Some will think of positive teachings from Jesus or the Buddha and picture such figures as the pope, Billy Graham, or Mother Teresa. But other things are also likely to come to mind.

The word *religion* conjures up images of destructive or even cruel behavior. Assumptions about religion now include violent actions rooted in intolerance or abuse of power. During the year following the attacks on New York and the Pentagon, Americans were inundated with media images of Islamic suicide bombers, Hindu fanatics attacking Muslims (and vice versa) in Northern India, and Christian clergy being arrested and escorted to jail on charges of criminal sexual misconduct.[1]

The title of the book from which this paragraph is quoted might as easily and appropriately been *When Attractiveness Becomes Repulsiveness* or—if it had focused more exclusively on the Christian faith—*How Christ's Captivating Bride Became a Common Whore*.

Should we ask your forgiveness for such shocking language as the title just suggested? Or shall we share with you the biblical text that suggests it? The Old Testament prophet Ezekiel reflected on Yahweh's relationship to Israel and likened it to choosing that body of people to be his bride. The Lord claimed Israel as his bride and brought her beauty to the fore. He bathed her, perfumed her, and clothed her radiantly. Indeed, she became "exceedingly beautiful, fit to be a queen"—and her fame grew (Ezek. 16:8-14). Yet Ezekiel indicted Israel for misusing the prominence and influence her (conferred[2]) beauty brought to her. "But you trusted in your beauty, and played the whore because of your fame, and lavished your whorings on any passer-by." Or as Eugene Peterson renders this verse: "But your beauty went to your head and you became a common whore, grabbing anyone coming down the street and taking him into your bed" (Ezek. 16:15 *The Message*).

As with national Israel, the church has not been chosen because of its natural charm, grace, and beauty; she has received both an attractiveness and a significance to others that has been conferred by grace. With the beauty given to her, however, her bridegroom desires for her to be seen resplendent in her loveliness—thus Paul uses terms such as "splendor, without a spot or wrinkle or anything of the kind." And just as the beauty of Israel was designed to turn the heads of other nations to Yahweh, so the attractiveness of Christ's bride is supposed to help the world appreciate his power to rescue, define, beautify, and ennoble. The church's grace, charm, peace, joy, and (resulting) *beauty* combine as the heavenly strategy to proclaim Christ's redemptive power to the world and to invite "whosoever will" to benefit from it.

It really is true that the greatest proof of God's love is an individual or corporate life that needs the transforming power of that love to explain its existence in this world! The church's beauty is therefore an evangelistic strategy. But it is failing by virtue of the misuse of her status and the prostitution of her charms. In a word, the church that has been seen as punitive toward outsiders and legalistic with insiders—all the while drunk on abusive power and living in denial—needs to sober up. Get healthy. Clean up its act. Establish a better reputation. Live from a purer character. Look more like a bride who is fit to be a worthy partner to her divine companion. Become attractive again. And turn heads toward her beloved.

The primary function of the church is not—as has become customary to affirm—evangelism. Rather, the church exists to demonstrate the inbreaking of the kingdom of God into human experience. To be a second incarnation of the divine presence in the world. Or, put another way still, *to be joyous, radiant, and breathtakingly beautiful by the fruitful presence of the Holy Spirit*. We will claim that beauty and joy constitute the divine strategy for making known the presence and power of God. And since what we have come to refer to as the church universal cannot be experienced as an abstraction, this beauty and joy must be received, experienced, and exhibited in communities of faith we call local churches. The abstract universal church can only be known in a congregation of believers that is a microcosm of the whole.

## Beauty as Divine Strategy

Why did people fall all over themselves to get glimpses of Jesus? Climb trees to see him? Hang on his every word? It was the beauty of the kingdom of God revealed among them in his person. His gentle humility convinced them he would never hurt them. His approachability made them feel comfortable in his presence. They became excited about the things of God because he was in their midst. And something about the beauty of *his* life convinced them *their* lives might even become beautiful too!

Why did the earliest church grow so rapidly? While two men who preach might want to claim it was the power of apostolic preaching, the truth of the matter is that it was the beauty of the community formed around that preaching. What does it do to a city in our own time to see Christians selling their boats and Rolex watches to feed the poor? To see Christians moving among one another with joy and kindness? To witness their small-group meetings over bread and wine to retell the gospel—and to be invited to those tables? Do you say you have no idea the impact such a thing would have, for you have never seen it? That just may be why the Jerusalem church had so much impact and our churches have so little.

Luke says that the life of that original community created such a stir that it drew others magnetically into what the Christians were experiencing. The believers were not only "praising God" but also "having the goodwill of all the people" because of their beautiful presence in Jerusalem—and the Lord added others to their number daily (Acts 2:44-47). Those earliest followers of Jesus had been right. Following the pattern of his beautiful life had made their lives beautiful too. The bride's winsomeness was turning heads toward her companion—and drawing them into the community of faith formed around him and in his name.

What if our strategy for evangelism were not campaigns and crusades but community demonstrations of the reign of God? What if we gave up on three-day revivals in favor of whole-church faithfulness in righteousness, joy, and peace? What if local churches became such hotbeds not of scandal but of compassion, generosity, and spiritual wholeness, that they became magnetic communities within the larger communities of cities, states, and nations?

It still happens on occasion. Churches come alive by the power of the Holy Spirit. Word gets around that something is happening among those people that enables broken people to be whole. Outsiders begin showing up at whole-community events (e.g., worship events, service projects), gravitate at different speeds into smaller units of that community (e.g., study groups, prayer groups, house churches), learn the central message of the gospel (i.e., their experience has made them hungry to know what has formed such a community), and surrender their hearts and lives to Christ (i.e., become his spiritual apprentices).

> *Wherever ugliness is kept at bay, there the Spirit of God, who is the God of Beauty, is doing His creative and re-creative labor.*
>
> —Donald Coggan

This sort of strategy for communicating Christ to the world is the natural function of a healthy society of Christians. Specific events of preaching or outreach are not precluded on this model. But it is the nature of the community itself that is primary. A healthy church attracts those who have been wounded, violated, and otherwise disappointed by life. They simply "wander in"—or so it would seem to a casual observer—and are saved. The deeper truth of the matter is that lifting up Christ through the enacted word by a community of faith has drawn them to the Savior (cf. John 3:14-15).

Traditional church evangelism has understood "lifting up Christ" to refer to preaching. Again, while not wanting to do away with our careers as preachers, the event of preaching serves principally to obscure Christ if the body life of the church is not creating a hunger and thirst for the gospel. People under the influence of a healthy church want to know things like: What is going on among those people? Why do they love each other so? How do they sustain such involvement in the larger community to make it a better place? Why do they care about me and my family? Why are they so unselfish with their resources? Why are they willing to deal so gently and kindly with people whose values are so very different from their own? This is surely an instance in space and time of what some thought was only an abstraction! The "universal church" has been concretized as a "local church"—which all can experience!

If we can't visualize such a church, what a pity. For that is what churches are supposed to be—not the brittle, isolated, defensive little groups of angry and sad-looking faces that assemble on Sunday morning at 10 o'clock and dare anybody to prolong their assemblage more than an hour. But if we *can* begin to visualize such a community, we know *its life would need God's love to explain itself.* It would be a beautiful and healthy community. And no one could keep people from rushing to it with a frenzied passion that would confuse the church-growth experts and force Satan first to weep and then to mount an assault against it.

### Do We Take Religion Too Seriously?

The church of the twenty-first century is open to the criticism of being too institutional and too formal, too preacher-focused and too program-driven. It has failed to see that analyzing sacred text does not guarantee likeness to Christ but may instead produce wicked posturings and divisions. It has too many written rules of its own creation—and even more unwritten ones. It is too quick to exclude the very people Jesus tried hardest to reach. There is too much of the world's divisiveness, competition, and materialism in the church and too little evidence that the church is modeling self-control, peace, and love to the world.

One can make a reasonably good case that the church has taken religion so seriously that it has obscured the vision of Christ—both for itself and a watching world. Religion tends to make people obnoxious. It strips the joy and spontaneity out of people's relationship with God and turns it into what Peter called an impossible yoke of mind-numbing laws and spirit-crushing judgments. No less than Jesus himself ridiculed the repulsiveness of truth and mercy turned into an oppressive system of laws, rituals, and abusive power. Its chief practitioners in his culture were the scholarly scribes and conservative Pharisees. And while the Son of God was comfortable and laid-back with people ranging from party-goers to cheats to prostitutes, he bristled in their presence. He knew they were threatened by him and hated him. Jesus never threatened drinkers, tax collectors, or even people "caught in the very act" of illicit sex with warnings about hell. He did warn the scribes and Pharisees who had no compassion toward such persons and who had made God seem so stern as to be unavailable, however, of the severe judgment that lay ahead for them.

The scribes and Pharisees were Bible scholars. They read, studied, and interpreted the Word of God for others. They also took it seriously for their own lives—binding themselves not only to obey the Ten Commandments, but also the 603 additional commands they had enumerated from the Torah. More than that, they built barriers against the possibility of even being tempted to break the commandments of the Law of Moses. For example, lest anyone be tempted to break the rule against work on the Sabbath, they forbade a woman to look into a mirror on that holy day; she might be tempted to fix her hair or pluck a gray hair or put on makeup. They prohibited a tailor from taking needles home, for he might be tempted to repair a torn garment. They warned against....Well, you get the picture. These weren't bad people, mind you. They were motivated by sincere passion for Torah and wanted to do right. But what they failed to realize is that one can obey every commandment in Scripture and still be a monster.

The purpose of the Law of Moses was to teach people how to love Yahweh and one another. Those two duties summarize everything God was trying to tell the Old Testament church through the prohibitions, duties, and rituals enjoined in their Bible. People who really got the point of all those books, chapters, and verses of Holy Writ would have lived as Jesus did, practiced religion as he did, and treated people as he did. The fact that his life, religious practices, and behavior toward others stood out remarkably among the people who were generally regarded as Judaism's holiest representatives shows just how far they had missed the point of religion generally and Scripture in particular. Obedience to the commands of God is certainly not optional for a disciple of Jesus of Nazareth. Disobedience that is deliberate and willful brings one under divine censure and opens the issue of hell for discussion again. But observance of law can be purely external. It is at least theoretically possible for someone to keep the Ten Commandments, the total of 613 commandments the Pharisees counted in Torah, or the Sermon on the Mount as a code of rules and be a cold, revolting, and horribly unattractive person. Yet Jesus taught and modeled the fact that a relationship with his Father does anything but create cold, revolting, and unappealing souls. People who get the point of religion and obey God acceptably are those whose heart-orientation and life-behaviors reflect his nature with grace, joy, and compassion. In other words, the people who get it look like Jesus—not scribes and Pharisees. They attract people and make their hearts more open to God, truth, character, generosity, and love. They are beautiful individuals. Collectively, they are Christ's beautiful bride. They are his disciples who have lived with him long enough to know how to duplicate his lifestyle.

One writer has imagined a Jesus figure walking among us today as a woodcarver named Joshua. As people are captured by his remarkable and fascinating character, they begin to speak with him easily about subjects of real importance to them. One of them asked him our question in this opening chapter: What is your opinion of the church? Why has "church" become a dirty word? What do you think of religion?

> "What do you mean by religion? Do they mean the way it is or the way God intended it to be? There's a big difference you know."
> "Well, the way it is, the way the churches run it."
> "God never intended that religion become what it is today. Jesus came to earth to try to free people from that

kind of regimented religion where people are threatened if they don't obey rules and rituals invented by the clergy. Jesus came to teach people that they are God's children and, as God's children, they are free, free to grow as human beings, to become beautiful people as God intended. That can't be legislated. Jesus gave the apostles and the community as a support to provide help and guidance and consolation. Jesus did not envision bosses in the worldly sense. He wanted his apostles to guide and serve, not to dictate and legislate like those who govern this world. Unfortunately, religious leaders model themselves after civil governments and treat people accordingly. In doing this they fall into the same trap that the scribes and Pharisees fell into, making religion a tangible set of measurable religious observances, which is legalistic and superficial. In doing this they become the focus of religious observance rather than God, and it is their endless rules and their rituals rather than love of God and concern for others that occupy the people's attention.

> *Religion is like the vaccine that stops you from getting the real thing.*
>
> –Billy Graham

"Customs and practices and traditions then replace true service of God, and these become a serious obstacle to real growth in the love of God. If people take religious leaders too seriously, they become rigid in their thinking and afraid to think for themselves, and must always refer decisions to the clergy. Even as adults they will still cling to the religious practices of their childhood, and when even ceremonies and mere customs change they panic, because they have been lead to believe these things *were* their faith. With that kind of mentality all growth stops, because growth means change and

holiness means an ever-deepening understanding of God
and what he expects of each one of us.... .
"True religion comes from the heart. It is a deep relationship with God, and should bring peace and joy and
love to people, not fear and guilt and meanness."[3]

The Joshua of the Girzone books is hardly the Christ of the
Gospels. He is a multicultural Christ. He is more a world-religions
figure, in our opinion, than a replication of the historical Christ's
heart and life in a modern setting. Having said that, however, the
author is correct in helping readers grasp the unpleasant truth
that onlookers today have an image of the church more akin to
a menacing witch than a radiant bride.

**When the Church Enjoyed Favor**
But it hasn't always been this way. There was a time when
the church enjoyed favor and goodwill from the people around
her. There was a time when the *incarnate* gospel paved the way
for people to hear the *proclaimed* gospel—and brought people
to salvation. But the time we have in mind wasn't in our lifetime.
Nor was it in the early days of America to which nostalgia may
incline some of us.

It is true enough that through the centuries since the
Protestant Reformation the church has had more cultural status
than it seems to have now. At various times and in particular settings and locales, churches have had a better reputation than
they seem to have at the beginning of the twenty-first century.
Even in the early days of the United States, the Bible was the
most-read, most-published book in America, and churches were
considered a necessary and vital part of colonial life. The cynicism that now accompanies so many perspectives on Christianity
had not yet formed.

That being said, the power structures and struggles that have
come to dominate the church landscape were already present.
As Mark Noll points out in his book, *America's God*, the
American intellectual climate of rationalism, individualism, and
republicanism combined with the dominant Reformed Protestant

understanding of Christianity to generate some unhealthy results. When biblical interpretations clashed as they did in the run-up to the Civil War, this Reformed spirit became a liability. Within a Reformed hermeneutical framework, the only possible explanation for an opponent's persistently erroneous use of Scripture was the opponent's malicious intent to pervert the clear word of God.[4]

In other words, the pursuit of unity through common-sense reasoning joined with our passion for democracy only led to more and more divisiveness. Thus it is not to some pristine moment in American church history that we can turn to find better times. Neither is there some "golden age" prior to the Protestant Reformation, such as the centuries of the dominant—and dominating—Roman Church Empire of the Middle Ages that we can offer as a model. One has to return to the beginning—all the way back to the days of Christ's immediate disciples. Even then we must admit that Luke's portrait in those early chapters of Acts may be a bit idealized. At least from our own experience, his words sound almost too good to be true.

> Awe came upon everyone, because many wonders and signs were being done by the apostles. All who believed were together and had all things in common; they would sell their possessions and goods and distribute the proceeds to all, as any had need. Day by day, as they spent much time together in the temple, they broke bread at home and ate their food with glad and generous hearts, praising God and having the goodwill of all the people. And day by day the Lord added to their number those who were being saved (Acts 2:44-47).

It is notable in this canonical account, however, that the goodwill of *all* the people is short-lived. At the conclusion of the next scene, the power struggles with the religious establishment of Jerusalem begin (Acts 3-4). The goodwill is suddenly a narrower experience of the shared life in community enjoyed by those who believe:

Now the whole group of those who believed were of one heart and soul, and no one claimed private ownership of any possessions, but everything they owned was held in common. With great power the apostles gave their testimony to the resurrection of the Lord Jesus, and great grace was upon them all. There was not a needy person among them, for as many as owned lands or houses sold them and brought the proceeds of what was sold. They laid it at the apostles' feet, and it was distributed to each as any had need (Acts 4:32-35).

The opening scene of chapter five takes away even that more limited sense of harmonious living within the faith community when Ananias and Sapphira are struck down for lying to the Holy Spirit (Acts 5:1-11). They apparently wanted the community affirmation that likely would come from making a sizable contribution to the church—in the manner of Barnabas (cf. Acts 4:36-37). But their gift was not given in the *spirit* of Barnabas. They were concerned to maintain their financial security, held back part of the proceeds of the sale, and professed to be giving the total amount they had received. A new element of hypocritical good works was thereby introduced into the joyous spontaneity of generous giving—and marred the beauty of the first church's life in a way Sanhedrin opposition never would have accomplished.

The early church described in Acts is a community of believers empowered by God's Holy Spirit to continue the activity that Jesus began in his own earthly ministry. They are empowered to act in the name of Jesus, and they bear witness to the kingdom of God inaugurated in this world by the life and ministry of Jesus Messiah. As one reads through the material, it becomes clear that the community of disciples understands itself to be the living embodiment of Christ. They live out the teachings of Jesus regarding wealth and poverty. The sick are made well and the oppressed are set free in the name of Jesus. Salvation is offered to all who receive the good news of salvation in Christ Jesus.

In that transformed identity as Christians, as followers of

Christ empowered by the Spirit to be the body of Christ, Paul exhorts the Roman Christians: "If it is possible, so far as it depends on you, live peaceably with all" (Rom. 12:17). The writer of Hebrews tells his readers: "Pursue peace with everyone, and the holiness without which no one will see God" (Heb. 12:14). But the very exhortations themselves suggest that harmony with the world and with one another in the church was already not a "given" in their world any more than it is in our own.

## The Plan of This Book

In what follows, then, we do not wish to make yet another simplistic back-to-the-Bible plea. But we must be clear that we *do* insist on going back to the Bible. What we are calling "simplistic" is the notion that calling for serious examination of the Gospels and Acts is sure to improve the life of the contemporary church and make it more beautiful. There is considerable evidence that careful reading, analysis, and exposition may only succeed in making the church uglier—with one scholar's "certain conclusions" discounting those of another and setting individuals or even whole groups at odds with each another.

Neither are we offering what might be expected from us in terms of a back-to-the-first-century-church appeal. Which first-century church shall we propose to imitate? They were by no means uniform in mission, organization, or even theology. There was no perfect church in the first century—just as there is no perfect one today. So shall we propose to imitate a church abstracted from all the positive things we see in the various churches on the pages of the Acts? The composite church of each interpreter seems strangely similar to the one of his own taste or her own experience.

It seems unlikely to us that seeing either the Bible or the first-century church as an end in itself will be helpful. We will simply continue fighting over interpretations, tinkering with church structures, and playing the political games for which churches are so notorious. What we do believe is that the experiences of those early believers as they were empowered by God's Spirit to be the Living Christ to their time and place are still accessible to all who are empowered by that same Spirit to be the Living Christ (i.e., his spiritual body) in our time.

We believe there is much to be learned by focusing attention on the life of Jesus and the lives of those who first imitated Jesus in announcing the kingdom of God. So the study of the Word of God is indispensable—but that study must be undertaken in a spirit of deep humility. We believe that much of the turmoil in and around our churches today stems from unhealthy beliefs and practices that are more about human power and control than God's power and presence. The reputation of churches and Christianity itself in our time has more to do with human dogma and our need to control and dominate others than with the active God who has made himself known by becoming flesh and dwelling among us.

In the following chapters we seek to focus with fresh eyes on the God who announces himself and his great love for his creation in Scripture. We believe God is not passive but active; he created and he continues to create and to act within his creation. We will explore the mystery of God's communal identity as God the Father, God the Son, and God the Holy Spirit. We have no new formula to describe how he exists as Father, Son, and Spirit—this will be neither a theological treatise on the Trinity nor an exposé of previous efforts to explain the relationship. We simply want to take seriously the communal nature of a God who calls those created in his image (i.e., humans) to live in community with him and with one another. The God we proclaim created us, loved his creation

> *Christianity is not a momentary, instantaneous affair. It takes time, cultivation, work, perfection, reformation. The essential locus for that making of Christians is the crucible of the church.*
>
> —William Willimon

enough to die for it, and continues to love by empowering us with divine presence. It is in that context of love and presence that we begin to comprehend the meaning and activity of worship.

As worship announces our awe and wonder in the presence of the living God, we become inseparably linked by the power of his love for us. The presence of his love binds us relationally to one another (1 John 1:9ff). Jesus himself modeled the redemptive grace and acceptance of sinners and strangers, changing forever the definitions of "neighbor" and "fellowship." We want to explore the relational link of grace and love that we are called to embrace and embody for the world.

A community of faith that lives together in the presence of God (worship) and embodies the relational links of grace and love will live in conversation. Communication (verbal and non-verbal) is the tie that binds humans to one another and to God in wholesome relationship. We cannot sustain any relationship without the encouragement of words and actions that communicate. Healthy churches—and healthy individuals who are their constituent members—sustain health and grow toward spiritual maturity through healthy communication with God and one another.

The church must remember that it came into existence as an expression of "Good News." What we are to communicate to one another and to the world is gospel—the Good News of God's grace, his redeeming love and empowering presence. Our source for that story, obviously, is Scripture. Much has been written about the authority of Scripture and our need to find "book, chapter, and verse" and to "speak where the Bible speaks and be silent where the Bible is silent." However, to paraphrase Jesus' words about humans and the Sabbath (i.e., "The Sabbath was made for man, not man for the Sabbath"), we would affirm that the Bible was made for the Story, not the Story for the Bible.

It is the Good News of God and God's activity that has authority over our lives, not the Bible *per se*. The Living Word does not stand pointing to the Written Word as our salvation, hope, and authority so much as the Written Word points to the Living Word as our salvation, hope, and authority. We believe it is time to rethink our strategies for reading and communicating the story so that God is the authority over our lives, not a particular translation of the Bible. Too many abuses of people and too many fragmenting divisions have sullied the reputation of Christ's bride because we became confused and deified a translation or some human interpretation of a particular text. In the meantime, the Christ who could have been known through any translation and in spite of flawed interpretation was missed altogether.

When the Good News of God's love is the focus of our proclamation and the story revealed in Scripture is embodied in the lives of faithful witnesses, we believe that joyous service to the world and to fellow believers will be a natural outcome. Evangelism will not be a method or strategy or even a particular ministry. It will be the life of the church. In turn, church will not be a place where people come to escape the world—as on a cruise-ship vacation. Instead, church will be a people prepared to do battle with the principalities and powers that threaten to deny our freedom with one another and our access to God-presence. Christians must learn again who the real enemy is and what the real goal of earthly existence is.

The church is called to be the Living Temple of God by the Holy Spirit. We are to see ourselves as a people living as aliens and strangers—pilgrims on a journey whose destination is not of this world. We are called to be living hosts to God-presence. We are the bride of Christ; we also are the living body of Christ. We are to be Jesus to our world. And the same attitude toward and treatment of the world that made Jesus appealing to those who were seeking God will have a similar effect when found in the life of his spiritual body, the church.

## Organic Models

If we are the Living Temple of God, if Christ dwells in us, and if we are the expression of Christ on Earth in the twenty-first century—if that is indeed our identity as church—then we must think of ourselves *organically* rather than *organizationally*. So many models and structures that we use both to describe and to function as church have been borrowed from the mechanical structures and flow charts of modern institutions. Too often we think of church more as a business than as a living organism, the host of God-presence on this earth. It is that institutional method and model of church that has become so justifiably despised and rejected in our time. It is that method and model of church that has hidden the Good News behind layers of bureaucracy and burdens of guilt and hierarchical structures of power, control, and church politics that objectify, divide, and destroy the very people for whom Christ died. It is that Living Temple that we seek to experience afresh through this study.

The calling of the church in every generation is to be less a debating society than a hospital. Less a prep school than a summer camp. Less a throng of social critics than people who know how to enjoy a life. Less an exclusive club than one so inclusive that it may be embarrassing to be on its roster. Less a location and its buildings than a people and their positive presence in a community. Less a convention of Ebenezer Scrooges than the get-together of a happy family. Less a bunch of fussy Bible scholars than a smiling clan going through its family scrapbook.

*We admit we don't know how to put it into words!* We are struggling to offer a series of metaphors that just might trigger an image in your mind that matches the one we were supposed to get from Scripture but somehow seem to have missed. We want to evoke an image that is relational rather than institutional. We would like for you to think family rather than big business. We want you to think of Christ in corporate expression but not as a corporation. We want you to think in terms of the direction of your life rather than your most recent failure or success. We certainly want you to think of faithfulness to God in terms of Jesus' emphasis on relationships rather than rules. We want you to sense that your own faith needs to be dynamic, growing, and maturing every day rather than worried because you don't have everything fixed, nailed down, and perfected. We're trying to get those things fixed in our minds too.

We want you to know the God who values you for who you are and not for what you can perform or give him. We want you to have a relationship with God as your Loving Father rather than religion's Wrathful Despot. We want you to know Jesus Christ as the faithful teacher who said that Sabbath laws were made for man, not the other way around. We want you to know the Jesus who said that his Father has more patience with a prodigal son or daughter than with a critical, self-righteous child. We want you to know the Holy Spirit not as the lost-and-confusing member of the Godhead but as the empowering presence of God for your life. We want you to exhibit the Spirit's gentle fruit of love, joy, patience, and peace as your contribution to the total beauty of Christ's bride, the church. We pray for and want these things in all our hearts and lives.

We believe that the kingdom of God is supposed to be breaking into this world through the church. But we must understand that it happens only when the gospel is enacted as well as preached among us. It is the real-life implementation of the Good News that makes its verbal presentation believable among those who hear it. It is, in fact, its enactment in a given faith community that will permit unbelievers to listen to what they may have already rejected because of exploitation, meanness, or downright ugliness in the church. The church needs to be saved from such a negative image. But to save her from such an "image," she must be saved from such behaviors through repentance.

### The Beauty of Relational Faith

An illustration of the transition we are experiencing from "scientific" models of Modernity to "relational" models in Postmodernity comes from the writing of a clinical psychologist. Several prominent child psychiatrists and some child-care institutions in the early twentieth century were enamored with white-coat care, minimal handling of infants to prevent the spread of infections, feeding from a propped-up bottle rather than by bacteria-bearing human hands, etc. It seemed so scientific and proper. But it was producing tragic results.

Infants subjected to these impersonal environments suffered emotional deprivation, formed no personal attachments, and did not thrive. Many died.

It had been reported, for instance, in 1915 that infants
admitted to ten asylums in the eastern United States had
mortality rates of from 31.7 percent to 75 percent by the
end of their second year. In 1920 a German medical
journal reported that in one of the great foundling
homes of Germany seven of ten infants died in their first
year. Although conditions had greatly improved, particularly in the realm of hygiene and nutrition, there was
still a 10 percent mortality rate in the best European and
American institutions. The condition leading to death
was sometimes called hospitalism, or failure to thrive,
and seemed to be accompanied by what looked like
depression and lost hope.[5]

Researchers such as Harry Bakwin began to ask the appropriate questions: Why do infants in hospitals fail to gain weight
when fed a diet babies thrive on at home? Why do they sleep
less, smile rarely, hardly make sounds? Why do they seem listless? Why don't they respond to smiles—even to touch? Why do
they look so uniformly unhappy? The world saw the same phenomenon on display in 1990 when camera crews went into the
state-run orphanages Nicolae Ceaucescu had maintained in
Romania. More emerged later in the decade as life in parts of the
Old Soviet Union went on display. Warehoused infants were
docile, lethargic, unhappy, and underdeveloped for their age—
even if they had food and medicine. Why?

Bakwin's theory was that children are relational beings who
need to form natural bonds of attachment in order to develop
properly. So he did something about it.

When Bakwin took over the pediatric unit at Bellevue in
1931, he changed the routines. He took down the old
signs emphasizing antisepsis ("Wash your hands twice
before entering this ward"), and put up new ones: "Do
not enter this nursery without picking up a baby."
Nurses were instructed to fondle babies periodically and
to sit them on their laps. Infection rates went down.[6]

Children began to thrive again. Human touch gave something equally as important as food, medicine, and cleanliness. Emotional bonding not only allowed but enabled talking, laughing, and mental development. Harold Skeels, a researcher who first noted the language deficits of children in settings without emotional warmth, wondered if something so basic as loving attention had an effect on intelligence. Could something that more nearly resembled mothering help?

> *To [God] be glory in the church and in Christ Jesus to all generations, forever and ever.*
>
> —Ephesians 3:21

This question led to Skeels' most original and daring study. He placed thirteen institutionalized children, all under the age of two and a half, in a home for older feeble-minded girls. The children were each "adopted" by one of the older girls (or in some cases by an attendant), who took over many typical mothering functions. The touching simplicity of this study lay in the fact that the retarded but affectionate girls proved in these circumstances to be adequate surrogate mothers for children this age. Over a mean span of nineteen months the average IQs of the maternally deprived toddlers in their care rose from 64 to 92. Seven of the thirteen were later adopted by outside families, where they maintained their intellectual functioning. Some thirty years later, when Skeels received the Joseph P. Kennedy Award in belated recognition of his work with disturbed and retarded children, he was introduced by a well-spoken, tuxedoed young man with a master's degree. He reported that he had been one of those children, depressed, withdrawn, deteriorating, "who sat in the corner rocking." As part of Skeels' study, he had been given over to a retarded girl for care and later adopted.[7]

Isn't *that* beautiful! And it serves to reply to one of the objections we can imagine readers making to the thesis of this chapter. How can a less-than-beautiful church like mine foster beauty? How can a bride whose own development has been retarded foster spiritual joy, peace, and growth? We have an answer in the famous experiment with "feeble-minded" surrogates nurturing "retarded" infants. In the context of a community under God, the Holy Spirit is able to do something beyond "scientific" or reasonable expectations.

There is an axiom in mathematics that a sum cannot be greater than its parts. While we don't particularly care to explore it as a math principle, we definitely want to challenge the notion that it holds true for relationships. We have both been present in too many groups—some large and some small—where things happened that were beyond the combined powers of the persons present. Cowards have become bold. Liars have become truthful. Defeated and dispirited people came alive and found a reason to live. It sometimes happens in families. It happens in therapy groups and in Alcoholics Anonymous. And it sometimes happens in the one place above all others where it should be taking place—in local churches. For in the church one has not just the interaction of human spirits but the presence of and potential for supernatural activity by the Holy Spirit as well.

Even less-than-beautiful churches can come alive, thrive, and display the beauty of Christ. Legalistic churches. Liberal churches. High churches. Low churches. Evangelical churches. Pentecostal churches. Dead churches. The power of God is able to awaken, empower, and beautify any body of people that will pursue a love-relationship with the Son of God and the people he cared about during his ministry—and think less about how things have always been or what somebody in this church or the larger denomination will think.

> Christ's bride is the church—people in relationship to one another. God has designed your relationships with other Christians as the primary contest [sic] in which His nature surfaces and becomes an observable, tangible

phenomenon. Not many nonbelievers are reading the revelation of God's graces revealed in Scripture. Many are reading the revelation of God revealed in your life and relationships. Like it or not, Scripture calls us *living epistles*, read (as a book) by all men. We are literally "Bible translators" for lost people.[8]

Aldrich points out that the church often weakens its ability to have influence on the world because of the "imbalance" that often exists between the verbalization and the incarnation of the gospel, our attempts at preaching it and our exhibition of its beauty. What he calls the "music" of the gospel must go before the preaching of the gospel and create a holy hunger for what will come through the spoken word. "The *music* of the gospel is the beauty of the indwelling Christ as lived out in the everyday relationships of life."[9]

It is the perfect plan. According to Paul, God is to receive glory "in the church and in Christ Jesus to all generations, forever and ever" (Eph. 3:21). Do you think Paul is referring to two sources? Or one? We believe it is two who have become one in the holy relationship of spiritual unity wherein the bride and her groom are to reflect glory to God in their pure relationship. As they move to the music of the harmony between them, the happy couple lives together in loving relationship—Christ and his redeemed people. As he leads, the bride follows. As people hear the music, the movement makes sense. As they look more closely, they see the bride's radiance and joy. And they are drawn to Christ.

## Conclusion

There is an ancient rabbinic tale about a wealthy family whose son was getting married. In order both to celebrate the marriage and to share their blessings with the people of their village, this good family decided to hold a great wedding festival. So they sent invitations to people all over their village and invited them to take part in their joy.

The family home was rearranged to accommodate the guests.

It was decorated beautifully. They set a generous buffet. They hired a group of musicians and set up a place in the corner of their spacious house where they could play. Soon the entire house was filled with music, dancing, and joy—as a happy family treasured the smiles on the faces of their happy guests. As they were dancing, a man who was deaf passed by the expansive front window of the house. He saw people leaping and smiling, whirling and clapping their hands, waving their arms in the air. But his handicap made it impossible for him to hear the music. And he would not go inside to investigate. So he made a judgment about what he saw. "Look at all that frenzied commotion!" he said to himself. "That must be the house of a madman."

So the poor man went on his way—neither willing nor able to take part in the celebration, for he could not hear the music that had stirred the wedding guests to such excitement and bliss.

## Notes

1. Charles Kimball, *When Religion Becomes Evil* (San Francisco: Harper, 2002), p. 16. "In their origins and their core teachings, religions may be noble, but how they develop almost invariably falls short of the ideal. Adherents too often make their religious leaders, doctrines, and the need to defend institutional structures the vehicle and justification for unacceptable behavior" (pp. 32-33).

2. Ezekiel makes it clear that Yahweh did not choose Israel as a bride because of her natural beauty. He chose her by an act of gracious love and beautified her. He did what we now call an "extreme makeover" on her—giving what she did not possess on her own. Cf. Deut. 7:6-8.

3. Joseph F. Girzone, *Joshua* (New York: Collier Books, 1987), pp. 73-75.

4. Mark Noll, *America's God* (Cambridge: Oxford Press, 2002), p. 379.

5. Robert Karen, *Becoming Attached* (New York: Oxford University Press, 1998), p. 19.

6. Karen, *Becoming Attached*, p. 20.

7. Karen, *Becoming Attached*, p. 22.

8. Joseph C. Aldrich, *Life-Style Evangelism* (Portland, OR: Multnomah, 1981), p. 36. The apparent typo in this quotation may be either a Freudian slip or an unintentional spiritual insight. The context for spiritual life in community sometimes is a contest of wills for power and control. Sometimes it is the struggle of an abused person to survive the abuser. Often it is simply the discouraging prospect of trying to pursue beauty and joy in a sterile institution whose identity is easier to maintain without the "messiness" of having to get along with unpleasant people. In Jesus' understanding, however, that very issue is at the heart of knowing God and experiencing spiritual transformation.

9. Aldrich, *Life-Style Evangelism*, p. 20.

The expression of Christian character is not good doing, but God-likeness. If the Spirit of God has transformed you within, you will exhibit divine characteristics in your life, not good human characteristics. God's life in us expresses itself as God's life, not as human life trying to be godly. The secret of a Christian is that the supernatural is made natural in him by the grace of God.

—Oswald Chambers

# 2. CLEARER VISION FOR THE CHURCH

---

*All of us, with unveiled faces, seeing the glory of the Lord as though reflected in a mirror, are being transformed into the same image from one degree of glory to another; for this comes from the Lord, the Spirit.*

—2 Corinthians 3:18

In the last fifteen years—at least among churches that aspire to grow and become in our cultural surroundings—the word *vision* has run a close second to *community* in conversation and writing. If a minister or church leadership team was interested in church growth, the expert advice was unanimous: "Your congregation needs to have vision. You need to take your congregation through the process of writing a vision statement or a mission statement. You need a concise way of describing the identity of your church so that people own the vision and aspire to it and invite others to join in. If you want your church to move beyond the complacency of the moment you have to inspire them, give them an invigorated portrait of the church and what God wants us to be."

Most of us in full-time ministry got about the business of convincing our leadership team that the church needed to write a vision or mission statement. The response among church leaders and members was often less than affirming of the idea. Some said it was a pointless exercise; the mission or vision of the church was already stated in Matthew 28: "Go into all the world and preach the gospel, baptizing them in the name of the Father, Son, and Holy Spirit, teaching them to observe all things that I've commanded you." The job of the church was evangelism; the preacher's job was to evangelize. "So get to it!" they said.

Others recognized that evangelism was not as simple as that, either for the preacher or anyone else. Right or wrong, much of life we have experienced in church settings is not evangelism *per se*. It is more often about nurturing the faith of those who already believe or ministering to those not yet ready even to talk about church or tithing or Sunday School attendance. Maybe our definition of evangelism was too small, but we intuitively knew that having a vision that was unique to our particular congregation did have some value. What was it that God was calling our congregation to become? Among all the other churches out there, what was *our* calling? Didn't it make sense to create a statement envisioning that calling?

So we read the stories and books authored by pastors at the big, growing churches and we imitated their mission and vision statements. Once we wrote the statements, we printed them for the entire congregation and told them, "This is the vision of what we want to be and who we want to become." We asked them to own the vision. At the first church where one of us went through this process, we had a special retreat for the ministry staff, elders, and deacons where we went off for two days and talked and prayed and wrote rough drafts. Then we rewrote and finally produced a succinct statement. We brought it back to the congregation and announced it. Everybody seemed genuinely enthusiastic about the statement. A series of sermons on the vision statement followed. People seemed to like the sermons. Then we waited for great things to happen. But instead of growing, the congregation began to experience decline. And we wondered about the "magic" that was supposed to be inherent in the vision statement.

## Whose Vision? Whose Church?

Both of us have experienced such "vision-casting efforts" in churches we have served. No, the results were not always negative as demonstrated through decline. But we also didn't experience the magical growth that the church growth experts had predicted. It was like praying for miraculous gifts of the Spirit and not getting them. We were tempted to decide it must be a lack of faith on our part. Were people not "owning" the vision? Was it just a bad vision statement? Didn't we ask God to bless our efforts, bless our vision?

A standard feature in almost every article and book on the subject of vision-casting and mission statements is a single biblical quotation from the Old Testament: "Where there is no vision, the people perish" (Prov. 29:18). One book noted that the version in use was the King James Version, a puzzling fact since all of the other quotations in the same volume came from the New International Version. When one actually begins to look at other translations, though, the selection of the KJV starts to make sense. In other renderings, the verse seems to be making a completely different point! For example, the New International Version reads, "Where there is no revelation, the people cast off restraint." And there is a second half to the verse that no one ever seemed to include: "but blessed is he who keeps the law." The King James reads: "Where there is no vision, the people perish: but he that keepeth the law, happy is he."

The more versions one reads, the more confused one becomes about the meaning of the verse. The Revised Standard Version offers this: "Where there is no prophecy the people cast off restraint, but blessed is he who keeps the law." The New American Standard Version uses the word *vision*, but adds a footnote that says vision could be translated "revelation"; thus this translation: "Where there is no vision, the people are unrestrained, but happy is he who keeps the law." Eugene Peterson seems to capture the essence of the original meaning in *The*

*Message*: "If people can't see what God is doing, they stumble all over themselves; but when they attend to what he reveals, they are most blessed."

There are several interesting things about all of this. One is the use of half a verse to proof-text an idea about needing to write vision statements for our churches. Or, at least, it was the preacher's justification for offering the church a reinvigorating project around which it could rally for the coming year. That particular half of a verse comes from Proverbs, admittedly a book in Scripture that catalogs "conventional wisdom"—something that is usually true, but not always.

> *A man with the vision of God is not devoted simply to a cause or a particular issue but to God himself.*
>
> —Oswald Chambers

Admitting that this verse is offering conventional wisdom rather than divine mandate, there is a still greater difficulty with the use of the KJV rendering. The "conventional wisdom" in this particular translation is garbled, if not altogether wrong-headed. Isn't it at least capable of being understood as a human vision rather than a divine one? A vision humans have for pursuing God rather than a grasp of the divine vision for us?

To say the least, its use in church growth seminars was a bit far-fetched. This text points not toward humans writing vision statements but toward the activity of God being revealed and humans being blessed to live according to that revelation. The original word translated "vision" in the King James Version is speaking about God's activity of revealing himself to humans, not the human activity of discovering, creating, or selling a vision for ourselves. This most definitely is *not* a text that says, "If a church can write a good vision statement, people will come."

From a cultural-historical standpoint, we can trace this vision statement phenomenon not to someone's reading of Proverbs 29 in the King James Version but to business models of success in the late twentieth century. Both in the business world and in some very large churches, this vision-casting—and the idea of a visionary leader who creates a new direction—had great success in the 1980s and 1990s. CEOs of large corporations—who owed a great deal of their entrepreneurial success to personal charisma—reshaped old companies into technologically updated and changed places with their vision-casting. "What is it that we do best?" they asked. The visionary leaders who answered that question passionately and correctly had great success. They became cultural icons. They made TV commercials, wrote books, and gave seminars to their peers.

Churches that approached growth through identifying their strengths and getting people to adopt those strengths as a marketing technique tended to grow as well. Having a vision of church that met people's felt needs, that celebrated personal salvation while giving people great worship experiences on Sunday did well in the 1980s and 1990s. Robert Webber refers to such churches as "pragmatic"—the vision-casting model had much to do with seeing church and the Christian faith as a commodity to be marketed.[1] Vision was the measure of the market appeal of a church. Vision was the motto designed to capture the imagination and offer the essence of a given church's marketing strategy. And there was a proof-text from the King James Version of the Bible: "Where there is no vision, the people perish." Those using this strategy successfully could point to all of the dying churches that had no vision. The visionary leaders who were able to ride the cultural wave of entrepreneurial management experienced success in growing large churches. They became cultural icons at Christian events. They made TV commercials, wrote books, and gave seminars to their peers.

## The Heavenly Mystery Made Known in Christ

One could argue that much more than a proof-text from Proverbs was involved in that model of church growth. In truth, many of the best models of management and leadership style found in the business world can trace their roots to biblical models and concepts. The ideas of leadership and management "from the bottom up" are inherently biblical. Evangelism is a process of convincing someone of a particular need—salvation. That sounds a good deal like sales. For that matter, due to government and taxation regulations, all local churches have to adopt some non-profit business structure and organization. Thus it seems only natural that one might find crossover skills and structures.

Without discounting at all the value of the business world finding models for leadership and organization that are compatible with Scripture, we would assert that every time a biblical concept goes into the world of business and then boomerangs back into the church setting, it brings some cultural baggage with it. It is difficult for a church wishing to have itself validated by campus size, offering totals, and attendance not to baptize the business model rather than actually engaging the biblical model directly. Business models invariably and instinctively include survival of the institution—survival and success of the product—as the primary goal. That instantly means competition with other products and clear differentiation of what our business does that makes us superior to someone else's. In other words, we have to surpass or eliminate the competition in order to thrive.

The question at hand is this: When the model for leadership and success is brought back into the church setting, should survival of the product or institution be the goal? We would argue that the goal of the church is not institutional survival but kingdom living. Our goal is be Jesus in our time and our setting. The differentiation involved is not about competition with other churches, but about bearing witness to the kingdom of God in our time and place. While many churches have thrived and grown large through appeals to a business-model approach, we believe the Christian faith is more than a marketing strategy to meet people's felt needs. Thus something more than adapting the models and marketing strategies of the business world must be at stake for vision-casting to have a role in the growth of the kingdom through particular faith communities called local churches.

Looking back over the past couple of decades, it seems obvious now that many churches and their leaders lost sight of a kingdom agenda for the sake of institutional maintenance. And the methods for achieving that goal were distinctly this-worldly instead of other-worldly in nature! All the while, we trumpeted the claim that the church existed as an alternative to the things that are hostile to God—by virtue of inveighing against drugs, sexual sin, and political corruption. But the voices were rare that spoke in opposition to doing kingdom things by worldly means and as measured by worldly standards.

It would bother us to visit the offices of fellow ministers of the gospel only to see more books on business management than prayer guides, more books of sermon outlines than good tools for serious personal study. Reliance on modern management and marketing strategies in our churches often seemed to abandon pursuit of the kingdom in favor of preserving our own institutions. Church conferences and journals were sometimes devoted more to attacking persons and churches than to exalting Jesus. Sermons often urged conformity to received tradition rather than inviting serious engagement with those who do not know Christ.

Can a church's measure of success ever be the "bottom line" of attendance, contribution, and property? These things may be consistent with faithfulness, but faithfulness will sometimes require that one or all of them be forfeited. If it is ever necessary to compromise the righteousness, peace, and joy that constitute the kingdom of heaven to get or hold them, the kingdom of heaven is being allowed to pass by for the sake of the institution's survival. Church leaders are merely doing crass institutional maintenance when they allow a church's life to be dictated by a grumbling member who gives substantial amounts of money rather than by the needs of the larger body, when they protect their status as power brokers rather than empty themselves as servants of all.

Think back to the previous chapter and its claim that "church" has become a dirty word for many people. Part of this can be accounted for by the fact that the church has not been an alternative to the world. Life by the world's rules is focused on acquiring and keeping power over others. Leadership is conceived on the model of giving orders and enforcing compliance.

Some form of winning a competition is the obsession that drives all decisions, relationships, and behaviors.

One who does church by the world's rules must have the final word and is willing to push others around. He struts in victory and pouts in defeat. She is seldom honest with others and never with herself. He cries for himself but not for others. She wants to be heard but cannot listen. He is angry and finds fault with all things and all people. She forgives nothing but remembers every slight—both real and imagined—that ever came her way. Satan's domain is filled with these non-kingdom souls who deceive, take, assault, and abuse. But the church is overpopulated with them too. They impugn, bully, threaten, and disrupt. By such means they maintain their cherished traditions and protect their institutional structures. And all these actions may be fully consistent with the vision they have mapped for being the biggest or fastest-growing church.

None of these things can be consistent with *God's* vision, which has been revealed to us in Christ. Love and peace, kindness and gentleness, patience and joy, humility and goodness, self-control and righteousness—these are the features of a vision for his relational community. They are the ultimate realities of the kingdom of God. They enflesh the two eternal marks of the church—love for God and love for others. So we must continue to pray for the divine vision with the words taught so long ago by our Lord: "Your kingdom come, your will be done on earth as it is in heaven." And we long to see flesh-borne passion for the preservation of human power, traditions, and institutions give way to pure delight in the sovereign rule of God.

### Vision as Revelation
As a matter of fact, though, listening to Proverbs 29:18 in its entirety may be a helpful beginning in the search for a healthier vision for the community of faith. But anything truly helpful will not be about memorable buzzwords and descriptive phrases that tell us what we want our church to be or become. Vision statements don't have to be marketing strategies. Such vision statements are invariably aimed at describing *human* activity.

This is what *we* humans are about at *our* church.

Such self-focused vision statements tend to sound like the following: We are a worshipping people at this church. We are lovers of God and seekers of truth. We are giving our lives to God and one another. We are known for loving God and serving the world. There is nothing inherently wrong with most of the vision statements churches have come up with over the years except that they have tended to describe human behavior rather than God's activity. They have tended toward descriptions of ourselves designed to be appealing to others. But what if we look seriously at the idea of vision as revelation?

Scripture gives us some incredible images of God's activity in and for the church. One of our favorites is Paul's description of his own ministry in the context of God's revelation for the church:

> This is the reason that I, Paul, am a prisoner for Christ Jesus for the sake of you Gentiles—for surely you have already heard of the commission of God's grace that was given me for you, and how the mystery was made known to me by revelation, as I wrote above in a few words, a reading of which will enable you to perceive my understanding of the mystery of Christ. In former generations this mystery was not made known to humankind, as it has now been revealed to his holy apostles and prophets by the Spirit: that is, the Gentiles have become fellow heirs, members of the same body, and sharers in the promise in Christ Jesus through the gospel. Of this gospel I have become a servant according to the gift of God's grace that was given me by the working of his power. Although I am the very least of all the saints, this grace was given to me to bring to the Gentiles the news of the boundless riches of Christ, and to make everyone see what is the plan of the mystery hidden for ages in God who created all things; so that through the church the wisdom of God in its rich variety might now be made known to the rulers and authorities in the heavenly places. This was in accordance with

the eternal purpose that he has carried out in Christ
Jesus our Lord, in whom we have access to God in boldness and confidence through faith in him. I pray therefore that you may not lose heart over my sufferings for
you; they are your glory (Eph. 3:1-13).

"This is the mystery of God now revealed to me and to all
humanity," Paul says. "I received this ministry by revelation. The
mystery hidden through the ages has now been revealed, so that
through the church the wisdom of God in its rich variety might
be made known to the rulers and authorities in the heavenlies."
Now there's a "vision" for you! God is using us to reveal his wisdom to the principalities and powers in the heavenlies!

Or think about Paul's language to the Galatians and the
Corinthians about the vision of humanity that he held because
Christ was dwelling in him. "May I never boast of anything
except the cross of our Lord Jesus Christ, by which the world has
been crucified to me, and I to the world. For neither circumci-
sion nor uncircumcision is anything; but new creation is everything! As for those who will follow this rule—peace be upon
them, and mercy, and upon the Israel of God" (Gal. 6:14-16).
What a radical understanding of his counter-cultural identity!

For the love of Christ urges us on, because we are convinced that one has died for all; therefore all have died.
And he died for all, so that those who live might live no
longer for themselves, but for him who died and was
raised for them. From now on, therefore, we regard no
one from a human point of view; even though we once
knew Christ from a human point of view, we know him
no longer in that way. So if anyone is in Christ, there is
new creation: everything old has passed away; see,
everything has become new! All this is from God, who
reconciled us to himself through Christ, and has given us
the ministry of reconciliation; that is, in Christ God was
reconciling the world to himself, not counting their trespasses against them, and entrusting the message of rec-

onciliation to us. So we are ambassadors for Christ, since God is making his appeal through us; we entreat you on behalf of Christ, be reconciled to God. For our sake he made him to be sin who knew no sin, so that in him we might become the righteousness of God (2 Cor. 5:14-21).

Seeing the community of faith with new-creation eyes demands that we focus on *God's* activity over our own. He is the creator, now re-creating in our midst, using his new-creation people as ambassadors, as conduits of his creative power in our world. We no longer view our cultural surroundings from a human point of view. We no longer view Christ from a human point of view because we have taken on an identity that is more than that. It is a new creation!

Consider the language of Jesus himself in that great last discourse in John's Gospel when he spends so much time talking about "abiding" in him. "Abide in me as I abide in you. Just as the branch cannot bear fruit by itself unless it abides in the vine, neither can you unless you abide in me. I am the vine, you are the branches. Those who abide in me and I in them bear much fruit, because apart from me you can do nothing" (John 15:4-5). He continues in the surrounding context to talk about the coming of the promised Holy Spirit who will teach them all things and empower them to love one another, to keep his commandments. Near the end of the previous chapter, Jesus had told his disciples, "Those who love me will keep my word, and my Father will love them, and we will come to them and make our home with them" (John 14:23).

Or consider the perspective found in Acts, when the disciples of Jesus are filled with the Holy Spirit and begin to do the

> *What matters in the church is not religion but the form of Christ, and its taking form amidst a band of men.*
>
> —Dietrich Bonhoeffer

identical works on earth that Jesus himself had worked in their midst. So many stories in Acts are repeat performances of the activity of Jesus. They perform the same miracles that he performed; they show the same concern to include all who once were seen as outcasts in the world. The church in Acts is the living embodiment of Jesus. Yes, because of human frailty, there are failures at times to be the embodied Christ, and Luke does not shy away from telling us those stories—Ananias and Sapphira, or the Greek-speaking widows receiving unequal treatment, or the looming controversy over the inclusion of Gentiles in the mission. But the vision of the church cast in Acts is a community empowered by the Spirit to be a second incarnation, to be the presence of God's reign on earth.

We have fellowship with God and fellowship with one another, John proclaims in his first letter. We are the dwelling place of God in the Spirit, Paul says. We are the embodied Christ. With that identity, the stories of Jesus himself come alive as models of church activity because Jesus understands himself to be the conduit of God's kingdom reign on earth. That's the announcement of John the Baptist when he says, "Repent for the kingdom of God is at hand." It is the announcement of Jesus when he is accused of being in league with demonic forces. "If it is by the finger of God that I cast out the demons, then the kingdom of God has come to you" (Luke 11:20).

So what would it mean to be a church *with* vision in the twenty-first century? And could we capture that vision in print? If by vision we mean the revelation of God being demonstrated through the embodied Christ, then whatever we're going to say will be about God and not about us. It is not even a matter of saying that we are a people who love God and serve others. That is still what we do. No, this vision must speak of what *God is doing*. This revelation indeed brings blessings to humans, but what we want to see and what we are called to reveal is God himself. What we want to envision is the Christ presence, the Holy Spirit presence, the kingdom of God activity that is using this particular community of believers as a conduit of God's new creation mercies on this earth.

We exist to live out the new creation of God. We are the Christ-embodied counterculture. We cannot be described by our buildings or our worship assemblies or our activities as would-be servants. We can only proclaim what God is doing through us, and we come together in assembly to share the stories; to identify with *the story*; to affirm our places in the story; to provide affirmations of the story through our eating and drinking—through ritual re-enactments of the story.

Or perhaps we could think of it this way. Rather than writing vision statements, we are seeking to embody the vision. The living body of Christ *is* God's revelation. Yes, we will use words to remind us of who we are. It is legitimate to speak of God's revelation through us. And it is legitimate to recognize and confess our moments when flesh looms larger than Spirit—both in our individual lives and in our communal lives. We do not yet fully live out the embodied Christ. We come into the assembly of believers to renew our eyesight—to put on new-creation glasses—that we might see ourselves, see others, and see all creation as God sees it. All creation groans in expectation for the consummation of this age (cf. Rom. 8). In the meantime, we will tend to creation and its creatures with new-creation eyes and minds and hearts.

## God's Vision for a Redeemed Community

Against the tendency of our contemporaries to interpret church out of our culture's academic, business, and other institutional models, we are convinced that the original idea God has for the church bears precious little resemblance to what church has evolved to mean for so many people—increasing numbers of whom are turned off to church. But neither are we ready to claim that everybody who saw the early church function was positively impressed by all they saw. After all, the New Testament tells us about some things going on at Corinth that Paul admitted were shameful even to pagans.

But there are also those wonderful texts saying that the Jerusalem church enjoyed "the goodwill of all the people" because of its rich sense of community (Acts 2:47a). Specifically,

Luke tells us they saw the Christians selling possessions, distributing funds to their neediest members, and enjoying being together. The passion those believers had for Jesus connected them to one another, created a sense of partnership, and forged a community of radical love. Tertullian (*ca.*160-*ca.*230) wrote that unbelievers of his time made this comment about the church: "See how these Christians love one another!"

Christians should make headlines like that today, don't you think? So *The Tennessean* would carry a lead story under the headline "Christians of Middle Tennessee solve homelessness problem" or "Feuding business partners yield to Golden Rule." Or *The New York Times* could carry a story titled "Terrorist abandons scheme; says 'Landlord's faith captured my heart!' " Instead, Bible Belt newspapers more nearly carry word of another church split. And terrorists indict us for spoiling their cultures with our materialism, pornography, and decadence.

> *Individuals cannot cohere closely unless they sacrifice something of their individuality.*
>
> —Robert Hugh Benson

If we could get closer to the original ideal for the church, there would be far less individualism, jealousy, and picking up one's toys and going home. Instead, there would be a healthy sense of community that would cause us to be forbearing, patient, and tolerant of our different points of view. In other words, we would be less a club and more a hospital, less a political party and more a family. Our world is profoundly fragmented by race, money, and power. There needs to be at least one place where people can belong, fit in, and be accepted. God intended the church to be that place. When God breaks in, things are supposed to be different! Accepted by God, we are supposed to learn to accept one another. No castes. No favoritism. No bullying. No discrimination.

Several years ago, a book came on the scene that said a

number of things we could visualize from our own academic experience. Reuben Welch said:

> For about a dozen years I've been a teacher at a Christian college in California, for the last five, I've been a college chaplain. I used to teach Greek—please be impressed— and every year we translated 1 John. Whether or not it changed many students, somewhere along the way it began to change me and I began to see words like life and light and love—especially love. And I began to feel John's concern for the Christian fellowship, and I began to understand his teaching that in Christ we belong together and we really do need each other. Then I became chaplain of the college—and the book came alive as I experienced the living needs of a living community not too different from the one John knew in Ephesus. I discovered that you don't produce community by bringing X number of warm bodies together and running them through registration. What a surprise to learn that compulsory chapel attendance does not automatically make us "one in the Spirit and one in the Lord." From the outside, it would seem that a Christian college campus would be a sort of anteroom to heaven—all these students in a similar age group with similar religious backgrounds and similar socio-economic status, and interest in Christian higher education and all wise—especially the sophomores. But I have found out, that in the midst of all these likenesses and similarities there can be fragmentation, division, insecurity, and loneliness—mostly loneliness. I also discovered that what John talked about was true, not only for some special group somewhere a long time ago and it is true for us right where we are.[2]

Registration and chapel and daily Bible don't suddenly create community for students at a Christian college. The school doesn't exist in some sort of vacuum, and the people on campus—both students and faculty—don't arrive in perfect condition. We all come with baggage. But Welch's words could as easily be applied to church as to school environments. There is a kind of "magical thinking" about church that is utterly perverse and harmful to those who embrace it:

- Thinking that the real world exists somewhere else and doesn't control or influence or degrade us.

- Thinking that in the church family, simply coming together once, twice, or three times a week will create healthy community.

- Thinking that everyone else at church but me is connected; everyone but me has friends, has a meaningful prayer life, and has their spiritual act together.

- Thinking with a "fix-it" mentality that believes community ills can be fixed with a new program, a new style of worship, a new staff member, a new method, or a new building.

- Thinking that social interaction will create spiritual community life. If we talk enough politics and go to football games and basketball games together and play a round of golf or keep each other's kids, that will constitute spiritual oneness.

- Thinking that sees all of the flaws in my current church and is sure that the grass is greener, the community richer, and the atmosphere more spiritual down the street or across town.

A trendy notion has come to the fore which says that churches can project community simply by using the word in their name. People are, after all, hungering for a place to belong, hungering for community; and the church is supposed to be community and we need to be more involved in outreach, in providing community. If we call ourselves "community," it will happen! But for true community to exist, something far more radical must occur. God must break in and do something stark, unusual, and supernatural.

Ironically, the hunger for community in our culture—and it is a very real hunger—lives in tension with the most dominant value of American life: individualism and *my* rights. One's individual freedom to choose *my* way, on the one hand, and the commitment to share common union/community with others are natural enemies of each other. The latter requires that individuals cooperate in ways that are often demand the decision to forego one's individual rights. We find ourselves desperately needing to maintain two values that are diametrically opposed to each other—the need to belong and share and have in common—*fellowship* is the Biblical word for it—and the need to be me.

Evangelical churches have insisted that one's "personal relationship with Jesus" was what mattered—not all of the tradition and ritual and stodginess of the church. At the beginning of the twenty-first century, the trendy vocabulary seems to focus on "spirituality." One can be deeply spiritual without connections to any religious commitments. And the pursuit of community is best done in other settings—the health club perhaps, a service organization like Kiwanis or Rotary, a small circle of friends from work. In the 1980s, television tried to convince us that community was best formed in a bar in Boston called "Cheers." In the '90s, it was those eccentric people who happened to cluster around Seinfeld or an amoral group of twenty-something "Friends" who had community. In our time, the real source of community for most people—at least while the kids are growing up—is their kid's school and sports activities.

Meanwhile, those of us with church heritage keep doing church, offering church to the hungering world as the true source of community, of fellowship—but our own dual-value system always seems to haunt us. Everyone has a right to his opinion about what every verse of Scripture means. Everyone has the right to choose how much we will give of our financial resources to the church. Everyone gets to vote with our wallets and our feet on every endeavor of the church.

In the larger world of Christendom, the maxim is that we all are free to choose the church of our choice. In pursuit of personal freedoms, Christianity is presented to the pagan world as a hodgepodge of names and buildings and doctrines and beliefs. And in the name of that same personal freedom, each of us can choose the place we think best meets our individual or family needs.

## The First-Century Challenge

The circumstances of Christians in the first century were not all that different from our own in some ways. People came into the church then from all kinds of pagan, dysfunctional backgrounds, and their baggage often carried over into the life of the church. Already Christianity was beginning to lose its sense of real oneness for the sake of following favorite individuals (cf. 1 Cor. 1:10ff). Already in the name of freedom claims were being made about moral and ethical living—the moral dos and don'ts of the faith (cf. Rom. 14:1ff). Already there were people claiming a new spirituality beyond any commitments to the historical existence of Jesus of Nazareth (cf. 1 John 4:1ff). Already community was fractured.

Our assumption is that those people just called a "new spirituality" group at 1 John 4 already had access to the Gospel of John. But their misunderstandings about the identity and teaching of Jesus in the Gospel had led to all kinds of conflicts in the church. First John is not a letter like the other two epistles we know as 2 and 3 John. For one thing, there is no particular person or church addressed.

> *As we realize that Christ lives within us, we also come to realize that Christ lives among us and makes us into a body of people witnessing together to the presence of Christ in the world.*
>
> —Henri Nouwen

It's a sermon, an exhortation. John believed that God had broken into history in the space-time event we call the Incarnation. He had experienced it and had been changed by it. And he believed the faithful proclamation of that message could create true community among alienated, dysfunctional people.

As you read the opening verses of 1 John, think back on the prologue to the Gospel of John (1:1-18).

> We declare to you what was from the beginning, what we have heard, what we have seen with our eyes, what we have looked at and touched with our hands, concerning the word of life—this life was revealed, and we have seen it and testify to it, and declare to you the eternal life that was with the Father and was revealed to us—we declare to you what we have seen and heard so that you also may have fellowship with us; and truly our fellowship is with the Father and with his Son Jesus Christ. We are writing these things so that our joy may be complete (1 John 1:1-4).

Community requires a basic set of shared beliefs and hopes and goals, if it is to survive, and John begins his sermon with a very crisp statement of a core set of Christian beliefs. There is a foundational belief, he says, that has to do with what has been seen and heard and handled—a physical presence *experienced* in the beginning that has issued forth in a word of life—a message that John wanted now to *proclaim* to his audience. It was a message concerning God's *activity* among them.

### Relational Faith

The core of Christian identity is not hermeneutics or a method for defining "inspiration" as it applies to Scripture. It isn't the frequency of the Lord's Supper or the fine points of baptismal theology. It isn't the role of women or what can be done from a church treasury. The ultimate "litmus test" for Christian community is the identity, presence, and transforming power of Jesus.

The power of this message that focuses on Jesus is that it gives life—but it is a peculiar (to believers!) kind of life. John throws us a curve here, for this proclamation is not about fixing sin and failure in the individual. He's not sharing this word of life so that individuals can experience personal salvation or a new spirituality. All of those things may be true of our experience of the Christ, but John says this message is being written so that his audience may have *fellowship* (i.e., may have a *shared* life, may enter *community*, may be *partners*) with him.

The plurals (i.e., not only the "we," "us," and "our" but the "you" and "your" are all plural here) are used by John to indicate a wider fellowship with others like him who have experienced this proclamation. Partnership with John and all those who share this "word of life" includes entering into a shared life with God himself. See the triangulation here? If "we" are partnered with God and "you" are partnered with God, then "all of us" are in a great and holy community together.

John could not conceive of relationship with God that is not at the same time relationship with other disciples. This Christian *koinonia* (i.e., fellowship, community, what we share) is formed by participation in the "word of life." One cannot make claims about relationship with God without also accepting the claims of relationship with the rest of God's people. Welch states it this way:

> Christians are not brought together because they like each other, but because they share a common life in Jesus and are faced with the task of learning how to love each other as members of the family. I'm sure you could not believe there is ever any tension in our home. There are four of us who live there. We have three children—two at home. We don't live there at our house because we just met on the street one day and decided we liked each other and decided to take up living together... .What brings us together is not our mutualities and congenialities and common interests and hobbies. It is not our mutual esteem nor our happy hormones—it is our blood ties, our common name and our common commitment—it's our parentage and our heritage and our bloodline and our life. And I think that is apt for the

church. So often we say "You ought to come to our church—you'd like us. You'd like our preacher, you'd like our music, you'd like our youth program. Come, please come, do come, you'd like us." And if they come and like us, then well and good. But if they don't like us, they spin off and we say, "Oh, too bad. They just never did seem to fit in, did they?" But you see, the church is not the society of the congenial—it is a fellowship based on common life in Jesus. It is the will of God that the Christian life be lived in the context of a fellowship of the shared life.[3]

Community of any kind begins with a decision to have fellowship, a shared existence with other people. The problem with Welch's family analogy is that too often people don't stay together because of common bloodlines and commitments—if the happy hormones are gone, so is the commitment to family. Individualism and my personal rights win out. Unfortunately that is even more emphatically true in the typical church setting. When the congeniality wanes, so do my commitments to community. John maintains in his sermon—the document we call 1 John—that any faith claims one has about God and salvation must be demonstrated in one's common union with other disciples. God must break in for it to be authentic spiritual fellowship.

Ernest Gordon was a British Army officer captured by the Japanese during World War II and assigned to help build the Burma-Siam railway. Men fed barely enough to stay alive were forced to build a track bed through low-lying swampland under threat. A man slouching or stumbling would be beaten to death or decapitated. Many simply died from disease, malnutrition, or lost hope. Fighting to survive, men lived like animals. They stole from each other. They robbed corpses. They hated their captors—and, for all practical purposes, each other as well. It was every man for himself! Then something happened that Gordon later called the "miracle on the River Kwai." God broke in!

A Japanese guard discovered that a shovel was missing at the end of a long workday. When no one confessed to the crime, he screamed, "All die! All die!" He put his rifle into firing position to shoot the first man in line. An enlisted man stepped forward and said, "I did it." The guard killed him instantly by crushing his skull with a rifle butt. When the tools were counted again back at the camp, though, it was discovered that a mistake had been made in counting. All the shovels were accounted for. One of the prisoners remembered and shared this Bible verse: "Greater love has no man than this, that he would lay down his life for a friend." And life in what had been a human hell changed overnight. With no formal prompting to do so, men who had been living as rugged individuals trying to stay alive began taking care of one another.

Gordon, so sick from typhoid, dysentery, worms, and malaria that he had been laid in what was called the Death House, survived because two prisoners made it their project to nurse him back to health. The transformation of the prison was so complete that, when liberation finally came, the prisoners treated their sadistic captors with kindness rather than revenge. Gordon later went to seminary, became a Presbyterian minister, and finished his career as Dean of the Chapel at Princeton University—where he died in 2002.

> The miracle on the River Kwai was no less than the creation of an alternate community, a tiny settlement of the kingdom of God taking root in the least likely soil. To a man, the prisoners clung to the desperate hope that their life would not end in a jungle prison but would resume, after liberation, back in Scotland or London or wherever they called home. Yet, even if it did not, they would endeavor to build a community of faith and compassion in the days they had left. For them, God was more certain than death.

> Perhaps something similar to this was what Jesus had in mind as he turned again and again to his favorite topic: the kingdom of God. In the soil of the violent, disordered world, an alternate community may take root. It lives in hope of a day of liberation. In the mean-

time, it aligns itself with another world, planting settle-ments-in-advance of that coming kingdom.[4]

So the soul's hunger to belong in community and to be spiritually connected to a Supreme Being turns out to be one longing—not two. To have one is to have the other. But to have either requires a radical shift in the fundamental value of existence and how we seek to live on this earth. Because of Christ, things have changed. We are not living a survival-of-the-fittest competition with one another. We are beyond individualism. We desire more than self-fulfillment. We desire the experience of Christ—to hear him, see him, touch him—in the experience of loving one another. Too idealistic? If it can happen in a World War II prison camp, it should not be impossible in the churches where we are! Or must the enemy trample us to within an inch of our lives before we can discover the love of God in one another? Before we learn the meaning of relational faith?

> *The people of God are not merely to mark time, waiting for God to step in and set right all that is wrong. Rather, they are to model the new heaven and new earth, and by so doing awaken longings for what God will someday bring to pass.*
>
> —Philip Yancey

Living with other people in fellowship means sharing all of our lives, not just sitting together a couple of hours each week in worship assembly. It involves someone else telling us how to live. It makes someone else Lord over self. It means letting go of our supreme American value of *my* rights, doing life *my* way. It means living as the chosen of God rather than making ourselves gods who chose what we want for ourselves. Life in Christian fellowship means discovering afresh each day that life is different because of what John had heard, seen, and touched in the Living Christ—and had been a partner in proclaiming to others. As people who believe that message, the challenge is to hear, see, and touch the Living Christ in our experience of one another in his holy community called church.

In such a community, not only do wounded souls get nurtured back to health but faithful witness is borne to people watching from the outside. There is goodwill from those who do not know Christ but whose hearts are prepared to receive the "word of life" from his disciples. It is as if the best answer to the question "How does one become a Christian?" is essentially the same as to "How do I become an artist?" or "How do I become a surgeon?" And that answer is this simple: Go to the community of people already about the task to learn from them, observe their ways, and imitate what you experience there.

### Conclusion

We don't want to be misunderstood at this point. We are not suggesting a Pollyana-type optimism about church and church life that glosses over sin and immaturity and insensitivity to one another and to our world. We firmly believe, however, that an understanding of our Christ-in-us identity and conviction that God truly is working through us will indeed create a radically different version of kingdom life and church than the one many of us have experienced. God chooses to see us through Jesus Christ, and he wants us to wear the same glasses when we see one another and the world in which we live.

As you read on, we invite you to turn in your old glasses, repent of your hardness of heart, and see the church as God sees it. See her not as a *leprous* bride—though we humans see all of the flaws—but as the beloved bride. Oh, that we might see with the eyes of Jesus, and hear the words of Proverbs 29 afresh: *If people can't see what God is doing, they stumble all over themselves. But when they attend to what he reveals, they are most blessed.*

## Notes

1. Robert E. Webber, *The Younger Evangelicals: Facing the Challenges of the New World* (Grand Rapids: Baker, 2002). See Table 2, pp. 17-18 for the remarkable links between the pragmatic, market-driven approach to church growth and the business world.

2. Reuben Welch, *We Really Do Need Each Other* (Grand Rapids: Zondervan, 1981), pp. 11-13.

3. Welch, *We Really Do Need Each Other*, pp. 26-27.

4. Philip Yancey, "The Least Likely Soil," *Christianity Today* (Sept 2003), p. 88; cf. Ernest Gordon, *To End All Wars* (Grand Rapids: Zondervan, 2002).

*Wrong thoughts about God lead to wrong worship of God.*

—A. W. Tozer

*If worship does not change us, it has not been worship. To stand before the Holy One of eternity is to change. Worship begins in holy expectancy; it ends in holy obedience.*

—Richard J. Foster

# 3. WORSHIP: THE CALL TO DIVINE COMMUNITY

---

*What to me is the multitude of your sacrifices?*
    *says the LORD;*
*I have had enough of burnt offerings of rams*
    *and the fat of fed beasts;*
*I do not delight in the blood of bulls,*
    *or of lambs, or of goats.*
*When you come to appear before me,*
    *who asked this from your hand?*
    *Trample my courts no more;*
*bringing offerings is futile;*
    *incense is an abomination to me.*
*New moon and sabbath and calling of convocation—*
    *I cannot endure solemn assemblies with iniquity.*
*Your new moons and your appointed festivals*
    *my soul hates;*
*they have become a burden to me,*
    *I am weary of bearing them.*
*When you stretch out your hands,*
    *I will hide my eyes from you;*
*even though you make many prayers,*
    *I will not listen;*

> *your hands are full of blood.*
> *Wash yourselves; make yourselves clean;*
> *remove the evil of your doings*
> *from before my eyes;*
> *cease to do evil, learn to do good;*
> *seek justice, rescue the oppressed,*
> *defend the orphan, plead for the widow.*
> —*Isaiah 1:11-17*

A major element of the joyous beauty of the Bride of Christ is surely wrapped up in the experience Holy Scripture calls *worship*. Yet it is painfully obvious from the words of the Almighty God that corporate human worship is sometimes detestable in his eyes. The very things he has commanded as worshipful acts can become an "abomination" to him. He can even come to the point where he "hates" and is "weary of bearing" convocations that have been called in his name. Therefore he will close his eyes and ears to what was meant to be beautiful, melodious, and holy before him. And don't you imagine that such worship would have long before then lost its glory both for the participants and onlookers who were supposed to meet Yahweh in the experience? That it would have become cold and formal? Or perhaps out of control and chaotic? Creature-centered rather than God-centered? Empty of any transforming influence on the participants?

If this horrible fate could befall the Old Testament bride (i.e., Israel) in her worship, it is not unthinkable that it could happen to the New Testament bride (i.e., the church) as well. But who can imagine a prophet being sent to utter Isaiah-like words to the modern church? Would we be willing to hear? Would that prophet be stoned?

We are convinced that an integral part of the beauty of the church before a watching world must be her times of public worship. But Christ's bride must not reserve the vibrant joy of her worship for Sundays or confine it to sanctuaries. She must learn what Yahweh attempted to communicate to ancient Israel through Isaiah—that prayers must correspond to behaviors, that a failure to defend the weak negates sound doctrine, that hands covered with the blood of injustice on Tuesday are unacceptable for bringing sacrifices on either the Sabbath or Lord's Day. Worship must be understood as a manner of carrying herself so gracefully that the bride is seen always to reflect her husband's personality. Worship and submission are inextricably related.

Somewhere along the way, Christian theology was detoured to the false, superstitious, and utterly pagan notion that one could be a career gangster yet have the favor of God at death through infrequent perfunctory confessions, occasional appearances at holy convocations on special days, or frequent generous gifts. If this sounds like mafia dons in *The Godfather*, it is also the celebrity athletes, movie stars, and politicians who use religion for show by hobnobbing with the dubious Protestant counterparts to corrupt Catholic priests and bishops. A watching world senses that something is terribly wrong in such an arrangement and sees ugliness. And the pomp and circumstance of a "lovely" televised funeral by either Roman Catholic or Protestant church officials is hardly enough to offset the negative image of a church that gives lip-service to one set of values and lives another. The unchurched and unbelieving world knows hypocrisy when it sees it.[1]

In this chapter we will search for fundamental insights necessary to a theology of communal worship that can make a practical difference in our life as a worshipping church. We want to avoid the "worship wars" of recent years, for the skirmishes in this ongoing crusade are more often about style and form in corporate events. We want to shift the emphasis to worship as the experience of God and others in community that is more encompassing than Sunday-morning corporate events. We believe such a shift would have the effect of enticing both disciples and nondisciples by its sheer joy and beauty.

## Stating the Obvious

The word *worship* traces back to an old Anglo-Saxon word that literally means "worth-ship." It has to do with assigning worth. In Christian worship, we assign ultimate worth to the God who made himself known through Jesus Christ. Thus worship is human creatures presenting ourselves before the Creator in whose image we have been made. It is our acknowledgement not only that we owe our coming-into-being to him or even our continuing-in-being but our very essence-of-being as well. That is, worship confesses our need to derive identity and function from the One who defines life as it is meant to be lived.

This fundamental truth about worship was stated by Jesus in his conversation with a Samaritan woman from the village of Sychar. When Jesus and the woman of Samaria talked about worship, the first thing the Son of Man told her was this: "Woman, believe me, the hour is coming when you will worship the Father neither on this mountain nor in Jerusalem. You worship what you do not know; we worship what we know, for salvation is from the Jews" (John 4:21-22). In his inauguration of the kingdom of God, Jesus sought to lift the eyes of both Samaritans and Jews from a view of worship tied either to a specific place (i.e., Gerizim or Jerusalem) or to a warped worldview (i.e., God as possession) to a perception which values God as immediately active in the world as life-giver (i.e., spirit) and life-definer (i.e., truth). "But the hour is coming, and is now here, when the true worshipers will worship the Father in spirit and truth, for the Father seeks such as these to worship him," Jesus continued. "God is spirit, and those who worship him must worship in spirit and truth" (John 4:24).

> The unique Johannine expression "The hour is coming and now is" brackets future and present without eliminating either. The saving sovereignty of the future is in process of being established through the Christ, and it is moving to its ordained climax in his redemptive death and resurrection, but not to its conclusion at that point, for the final resurrection is yet to take place, even after Easter (so 5:25; cf. 5:28-29). Since the kingdom of God is the age of the Spirit's outpouring, true worshippers will worship the Father in virtue of the life, freedom, and

power bestowed by the Spirit, and in accordance with the redemptive revelation brought by the Redeemer.[2]

Jesus shared a critical insight into the nature of worship that the woman of Sychar could not have appreciated on the day she heard it. The fact of the matter is, however, that the church across the centuries generally has not grasped his meaning either. Some focus on the word "spirit" and stress that worshippers must have a spiritual sense about themselves or a pure and teachable spirit in worship. Others give emphasis to "Spirit" and emphasize that worship must be animated by God's Holy Spirit. Both these claims are surely true, but neither seems to us to be the point Jesus was making. As to the word "truth," our penchant toward exegetical fervor tends to dwell on right teaching that corrects such misunderstandings about the nature of God as the Samaritan woman had received. For others, the need for "truth" is about correct forms and ceremonies in our worship events. Again, while both these points are undoubtedly true, they don't capture the deeper sense of Jesus' meaning in this conversation.

> *Worship helps us find who we are and why God has placed us here on the earth. When we bow in God's presence with worship, only then are we made complete.*
>
> —Judson Cornwall

That a single preposition introduces "spirit and truth"[3] suggests that we do not have two topics here to be broken out and expounded separately. It seems far more likely that worship "in spirit and truth" is supposed to point us to a single indivisible idea about worshipful devotion to the one Jesus—in language that may have shocked the woman and which certainly would not have been natural to her—called "the Father." Our suggestion is that there is a clear trinitarian view of worship here in which Jesus proclaims that the *Father* is not worshipped at selected holy shrines but everywhere and always through the *Son*—who is the truth (John 14:6)—and through the *Holy Spirit* who generates all spiritual life and whose indwelling presence changes everything.[4]

Christian worship, whether corporate or individual, is neither a place nor an act nor a prescribed series of acts but *an attitude of heart and life that reflects the experience of God*. Because of the interrelationship of Father, Son, Spirit, and worshipper, such communion is possible. There is genuine mystery here, and mortals must tread humbly on this holy ground! In a word, Father and Son are "one," believers are "in Christ" and Christ is "in" us, and Christians are personally indwelt by the Spirit and the church as a body is his living temple; the worshipful life appropriate to such shared presence overflows from a heart filled with wonder, love, and praise and shows itself in such familiar actions as prayerful entreaty, preaching the Word of God, and song or such unfamiliar (to us!) events as dance, lament, and drama.

We worship God because of his worth, glory, and majesty. As in the great worship scene Isaiah witnessed, we join the heavenly choir to proclaim: "Holy, holy, holy is the LORD of hosts; the whole earth is full of his glory" (Isa. 6:3). He is worshipped as the Creator God: "You are worthy, our Lord and God, to receive glory and honor and power, for you created all things, and by your will they existed and were created" (Rev. 4:11). Even more, God is worthy of praise because of his redemptive acts in history: "Salvation belongs to our God who is seated on the throne, and to the Lamb!" (Rev. 7:10; cf. 5:9).

Thus we are not surprised to learn that worship is a central part of Christian life and witness, that it is commanded of Christ's disciples. Neither are we shocked to discover that the neglect of it has disastrous consequences to a spiritual life.

## Stating the Not-So-Obvious

Christians are not expected to be worshippers for God's sake but for the opportunity it gives us to participate in divine community—and for the sake of those around us who will be attracted to and drawn into that community. It is an ancient pagan notion—one which Plato mocked in his *Euthyphro*—that a deity could somehow depend on its devotees. Perhaps the idea arose quite naturally among the Greeks because pagan idols had to be carved, transported, and adorned by their worshippers. Maybe some of that pagan sense of the deity's dependence on place and ceremony was involved in the Samaritan worship Jesus repudiated in his conversation with the woman of Sychar. And it seems quite possible that some of the same sentiment of a deity held captive by his followers crept into Judaism and its devotion to the temple ritual that was apparent in the time of Jesus and which also appears to have been a target of his words in John 4.

Whatever the history and application of the notion that pagan deities somehow depend on things from human beings, Paul repudiated it for the God of the Christian religion. Surrounded by the temples, altars, and statues of gods known to Athens in the first century, he addressed the fundamental difference between the *true* God who is an eternal and self-sufficient spirit being and pagan idols. "The God who made the world and everything in it, he who is Lord of heaven and earth, does not live in shrines made by human hands, nor is he served by human hands, as though he needed anything, since he himself gives to all mortals life and breath and all things" (Acts 17:24-25).

Is it possible that some Christians still have a semi-pagan notion of our worship? Do we ever communicate a theology of worship that leaves the *Euthyphro*-like impression that its purpose is transactional? We give *this* (e.g., money, prayers) in order to get *that* (e.g., more money, success)? To be sure, worship brings us before the Lord and invites us to reveal not our needs but our total dependence on him. As we pray for daily bread or deliverance from temptation or forgiveness, we have the absolute assurance "that if we ask anything according to his will, he hears us" (1 John 5:14). Surely we are to understand this much as we understand the relationship language of married love. But some people have so impoverished both contexts that they give flowers to get sex or offer prayers to receive fresh blessings; these are *persons making transactions*. Others give flowers to affirm the receiver as she is and pray to move their wills into the divine; these are *persons in love*.

God invites us to worship because of the healthy effect it has in getting our attention off the transitory things of this world and drawing us into eternal realities. Because this world so easily distracts us from heavenly things, worship reorients our thinking to what is true. Because the cares of this world can choke out the good seed of the Word of God, we must be challenged constantly to seek the things that are above (cf. Col. 3:1). Returning to the image of the church as the bride of Christ, the purpose of worship is to draw the church out of self-absorption into authentic intimacy with her Beloved.

Suppose we were to take the notion of *intimacy* between Christ as bridegroom and the church as bride seriously. If we were to do so, it might help us understand an important feature of Christian worship that we tend to slight, if not miss altogether. Human beings are sexual beings by God's creative design. As persons in God's own image, our sexual nature is important to the experience of community and becomes an appropriate metaphor for the experience of worship.

> Then God said, "Let us make humankind in our image, according to our likeness; and let them have dominion over the fish of the sea, and over the birds of the air, and over the cattle, and over all the wild animals of the earth, and over every creeping thing that creeps upon the earth."
>
> So God created humankind in his image, in the image of God he created them; male and female he created them.
>
> God blessed them, and God said to them, "Be fruitful and multiply, and fill the earth and subdue it..." (Gen.1:26-28a).

The critical thing about this text is not sex but *personhood*. All human beings bear the image and likeness of God. That we are both male and female in our humanity is not an evolutionary accident but a divine choice. It is obvious from this first biblical text about the subject that human sexuality allows God's image-bearers to participate with him in the act of creation. From texts that follow in Scripture, it is equally plain that sex serves purposes other than the generation of new life. Sex is a primary means for drawing humans into community with one another as families, friends, and covenantal partners.

At the beginning of the human experience in Eden, God was concerned to provide Adam a "helper"—not for work but for companionship, not for sexual gratification but for deliverance from social isolation.[5] Adam had animals for amusement and work, but he was "alone" in some significant way. "I will make him a helper as his *partner*," said the Lord God (Gen. 2:18b). When Eve was created, she was brought to the man and received by him as "bone of my bones and flesh of my flesh." The story ends with these words: "Therefore a man leaves his father and his mother and clings to his wife, and they become one flesh. And the man and his wife were both naked, and were not ashamed" (Gen. 2:24-25).

As two embodied persons, Adam and Eve were to become "one flesh." This language is not to be heard as euphemistic sensitivity but as a remarkable comment on the depth of commitment between two embodied persons who are essentially and vitally *different* in their natures. The union of a man and woman in marital sex is so complete that they can be thought of as having not two but only one body. There is certainly nothing negative toward human sexual expression in these opening lines of Scripture. The nakedness (i.e., vulnerability) of the man and woman to each other in their sexual natures was hardly a source of shame. It was joyous and celebratory—as that of the lover and his beloved in Song of Solomon. The union of persons "essentially and vitally *different*" cannot occur in homosexual experiences or so-called gay marriage. It can only occur across the natural barrier of male-and-female difference.

Because many of our contemporaries have long ago rejected the doctrine of divine creation, accepted that humans are simply a part of nature, and that our sexual urges are merely elements of our animal nature, they can affirm homosexuality as nothing more than an alternative lifestyle. They can define "sexiness" in terms of purely physical form, physical appearance, and physical performance. Thus "making love"—bridging the difference between male and female in the human race—can be abandoned for the sake of "having sex" or simply "doing it."

> *Our greatest claim to nobility is our created capacity to know God, to be in personal relationship with him, to love him and to worship him. Indeed, we are most truly human when we are on our knees before our Creator.*
>
> —John R.W. Stott

If we focus enough to grasp what has just been said about male and female personhood in marriage, we can begin to grasp another feature of the bride-to-bridegroom relationship between the church and Christ. In the relationship of a man and woman in holy matrimony, each is called outside of self for the sake of another. Indeed, each is called to become one with the other. The essential barrier of maleness to femaleness and vice versa is transcended through love.

Our sexually-based sense of incompleteness also forms the dynamic lying behind the search for truth, a search which ultimately becomes the search for God. We long to have our incompleteness fulfilled, and this longing gives rise to the religious dimension of life. The message of the Bible, beginning already in the book of Genesis, claims that in the final analysis the source of this incompleteness is found in the community that focuses on fellowship with the Creator.[6]

This view of human sexuality as fulfillment in another person through loving union has a direct and valuable application to our understanding of the church as the bride of Christ. Human beings are not whole within ourselves but long for the completeness that can only come from union with God. This is the meaning of a line from Paul that typically goes unnoticed and undeveloped in his discussion of sexual behavior in his correspondence with the church at Corinth. "The body is meant not for fornication but for the Lord, and the Lord for the body," he insisted (1 Cor. 6:13). This is due principally to the fact that Christians have been "bought with a price" through Jesus' death and therefore are obliged to "glorify God in your body" (1 Cor. 6:20). We know both these texts and employ them in teaching both young and old about purity. Here is the line that has not been developed adequately in our moralistic use of the same section of Scripture: "But anyone united to the Lord becomes one spirit with him" (1 Cor. 6:17).

Paul has just written about sexual union with a prostitute as a mocking form of bringing two human parties together as "one flesh" (1 Cor. 6:15-16). So interpreters typically rush by the comment about the union of believers to the Lord and our becoming "one spirit with him" in order to underscore his warning about the Christian duty to avoid sexual sin. But it is an important line for his theology—and one we have overlooked in developing our own.

If the sexual experience between male and female is designed to allow them to cross the barrier of their differences as male and female in order to be one flesh, how much more dramatic is the assertion that spiritual experience between deity and humanity allows a far more profound crossing of barriers! The essence of God is pure holiness, pure truth, pure love; the essence of humankind is not. Yet our human hearts long to experience the divine essence. We cry out for holiness, truth, and love. It is altogether impossible, however, for us either to create these qualities for ourselves or to surmount the barrier between ourselves and God and enter into these attractive traits of the divine nature.

So God took the initiative. The term we use to describe that initiative is incarnation.

> T]here is one God;
> there is also one mediator between God and humankind,
> Christ Jesus, himself human,
> who gave himself a ransom for all (1 Tim. 2:5-6a).

God condescended to our lowly estate. God—without sacrificing his divine nature—took on our humanity as Jesus of Nazareth. He was tempted but overcame. He was murdered but rose from the dead. Now he is exalted in heaven. And he continually pursues his bride to be "united to the Lord" and to "become one spirit with him"—to cross the barrier that otherwise leaves humans incomplete and unfulfilled.[7] To experience intimacy with one whose essence is different from ours. To know holiness, truth, and love in the experience of eternal life with him. Worship is the ongoing invitation to that experience.

### Knowing God

Because God created us for his fellowship and desires for us to live in relationship with him, the metaphor of the church as Christ's bride likely holds more promise than any other for bridging an understanding of "knowing God" that entails true intimacy. It is not enough to know *about* him, for what James says of the difference between dead and living faith could also be said of that (cf. Jas. 2:19). The demons know *about* God, but they do not *know* him. They do not live intimately with him. They do not experience his holiness, truth, and love. They have no share in eternal life. In the same way, we must be careful not to offer seminars, books, or "worship services" as alternatives to worship. To do so would be about the same as being a junkie for marriage-and-family workshops as a substitute for living as one flesh with a mate whom one loves devotedly.

A theology of worship for the church needs to begin with serious reflection on the nature of God. Specifically, it should begin with a careful study of the implications of the orthodox doctrine of the Trinity. Although the term "Trinity" is nowhere to be found in the Bible, the trinitarian formula of God as Father, Son, and Holy Spirit is found throughout the New Testament (cf. Matt. 28:18; Eph. 4:4-7; Jude 20-21). The words and actions of Jesus reflect the full consciousness of his redemptive work as a relational event in full partnership with the Father and Holy Spirit. Some of the impoverished theology of worship that has caused the church to languish recently may well trace to the fact that we have treated trinitarianism as an obscure footnote for scholarly reflection. We think it is far more crucial than that.

Are we bold enough to claim that we understand the triune nature of God? That we can explain it in simple terms? That we can trace out all its implications for worship—or any other part of the church's life? Hardly! We are attempting to claim in a very humble way that this difficult, mysterious, and ultimately inexpressible fact about God has practical dimensions we have often missed ourselves. But we do believe that reflection on this important doctrine will reshape our theology of worship in positive ways. The summary ideas we offer here certainly need to be traced out more fully than the purpose of this book demands or allows.[8]

## God in Relationship

An orthodox theology of the Trinity reveals a God in relationship. Altogether unlike Aristotle's singular Unmoved Mover who somehow creates order in the cosmos by having all things move toward him—while he/it dwells in splendid isolation and reflects on him/itself—the God of Christian faith is social. Revealing himself in undifferentiated form as Yahweh in the Old Testament, he is known in the Gospels and New Testament epistles as a single essence (i.e., level of being) engaged in both internal and external relationships as God the Father, God the Son, and God the Holy Spirit. It is here that we often use the word "mystery" as we fumble to grasp the notion of a deity who is completely one but who is somehow three distinct entities.

Christians do not believe there are three Gods. That would be polytheism as opposed to monotheism. Orthodox Christians are staunchly monotheistic yet affirm that the God who is one in divine essence exists in three separate personalities. God is one, and there is no God but the Holy Trinity; God is Father, Son, and Holy Spirit.

We believe it is grossly incorrect to offer an analogy for the Trinity such as water (i.e., a single substance) that can be experienced in three ways as steam, water, and ice. Nor is it adequate to say that the same person, John, can in certain relationships fill different roles—husband to Mary, father to Billy, and brother to Richard. The former fails to say anything of the dynamic relationships which are essential to the God of the Bible; it simply offers changes of form for the presentation of a single item. The latter seems more promising in that it is personal and speaks of relationships. It still offers no differentiation, however, and speaks only of roles or acted parts; it even smacks of a sort of deception to have the Incarnate Christ praying to his Heavenly Father and receiving authentication from the Spirit in the form of a dove, as took place at the baptism of Jesus by John (cf. Matt. 3:13-17).

There is no perfect analogy to express the divine nature, but neither are we left without hints and shadows. For example, if deity is a level of personal being higher than that of angel or human being, it should no more be thought impossible for there to be separate personalities at that supreme level than at the lower levels of angel (e.g., Gabriel, Michael, et al.) or human (e.g., John, Rubel, et al.). The essence that makes one an angel or a human is common, shared, and one; the human race is ultimately one (cf. Acts 17:26) though differentiated into many separate persons. Similarly, the essence of perfect holiness, perfect truth, and perfect love that makes one divine is common, shared, and one; deity (i.e., Godhead, cf. Rom. 1:20; Col. 2:9) is ultimately and necessarily one though differentiated as three separate persons.

Interestingly, marriage also gives a glimpse into the concept of trinitarianism. A human male and a human female are distinct personalities, minds, and bodies. Yet communication, love, and covenanting are possible between them because of the common essence (i.e., humanity) they share. In marriage, two personalities become one in a relationship of attention and mutual care. There is both diversity and unity at the heart of their covenant association.

These two metaphors begin to point us toward a critical truth about One God in Three Persons. That critical truth is *belonging*. Father, Son, and Holy Spirit exist as a community in which the activity of positive relationships presume and require communication, exchange, and esteem. The most important single defining relationship of that divine community is love—so much so that John can declare "God *is* love" (1 John 4:8). Trinity is the perfect community in which the ongoing dynamic exchange among persons gives the community its very identity. Father, Son, and Holy Spirit are so intertwined in a communion of love that one cannot be identified without the others.

In the Trinity, individuality is real. Each person is distinct from the other, but it is the mutual submission and reciprocity in love that is their communion. There is authentic unity in diversity. Thus it is the triune God who reveals the goal toward which a spiritual community—whether church or family—strives. It is the understanding of unity that is not uniformity, self-giving that is not diminishment, and love as surrender that is not loss that challenges the people of God to live as their social reality what the world cannot fathom in its defensive selfishness.

> Because God is the social Trinity, a plurality in unity, the ideal for humankind does not focus on solitary persons, but on persons-in-community. God intends that we reflect his nature in our lives. This is only possible, however, as we move out of our isolation and into relationships with others. The ethical life, therefore, is the life-in-relationship, or the life-in-community.[9]

### Worship, Community, and Relationship

What Grenz affirms about the ethical life of God's people is even more fundamentally true of the worshipful life of the bride of Christ. Worship enables people in the image of God to be self-giving by showing both devotion to God and dedication to their neighbors. When someone claims that "all of life is worship," he or she is likely trying to affirm the promise of the Holy Spirit's continuous presence. Any activity of our bodies also implicates not only the passion of our hearts but Spirit-presence in us. This is not to claim, however, that either life-as-worship or Spirit-presence is equal in all settings. Not all circumstances share the same degree of awareness of divine presence. Some of life is dull routine. Some is warfare against our souls by the Prince of Darkness. Some even plays out as a denial of Spirit-presence within us when we sin. Authentically worshipful life bubbles up and spills over into every relationship and activity. All things are sanctified to the Lord because of constant Spirit-presence. Thus even the dull routine, a time of crisis, or spiritual failure is ultimately sanctified to God (cf. Rom. 12:1).

Worship reminds the worshippers *who* they are and *whose* they are. We no longer belong to ourselves but to Christ. "I have been crucified with Christ; and it is no longer I who live, but it is Christ who lives in me," proclaimed Paul. "And the life I now live in the flesh I live by faith in the Son of God, who loved me and gave himself for me." (Gal. 2:19b-20). That being the case, we could not be surprised at this: "So then, whenever we have an opportunity, let us work for the good of all, and especially for those of the family of faith" (Gal. 6:10). The two commandments about loving God and loving one another always go together. One cannot worship acceptably who is otherwise unjust, doing evil things, or ignoring widows and orphans. This was Yahweh's message to Israel through Isaiah, Christ's to his contemporaries (Matt. 5:23-24), and John's to the church (1 John 3:17; 4:20-21).

When the church is together in her corporate worship, the proclaimed (i.e., preaching Scripture) and symbolized (i.e., eating the Lord's Supper) Word challenges the bride not only to be faithful to her husband but to make her love manifest in serving those in the community. The love that exists freely as self-giving activity within the Trinity becomes the model for how the individuals who are one in Christ will love one another. The corporate assembly overflows into the daily life experience of all who are in that relationship. Such love blesses even the larger community around that church. The bride's radiance turns heads to her bridegroom, and the world is captivated by the beauty of God's love that is being lived out in the church.

To say it another way, the truth that God is love means that it is in the very essence of the divine nature to be other-centered and self-surrendering. Again, think of the contrast of this tri-une God over against Aristotle's god who constantly reflects on his own perfection and immutability. When the ideal community of unselfish caring decided to create humans in the divine image, the new community on Planet Earth had a model for its life. We were created with the capacity to live in relationship, to be self-emptying for the sake of one another, and to experience the love of God through one another's presence.

> *If worship is just one thing we do, everything becomes mundane. If worship is the one thing we do, everything takes on eternal significance.*
>
> —Timothy J. Christenson

Into the world with such glorious possibilities came sin. With sin came competition, jealousy, and a new model that would corrupt authentic community. A monarchical concept of power emerged which depends on rigid structure, consolidation of influence, and exercising control over others. What a far cry from the trinitarian community and human life modeled after it. But this became the norm in human society and easily corrupts the way even a distinctly spiritual community is supposed to operate.

In the course of the earthly ministry of Jesus, he raised eyebrows and confused minds by speaking of a new way to exercise authority. In reality, he was only calling them back to the original plan of community. Unlike Gentiles—think of the Roman Empire and its hierarchical structures—who "lord it over" people, he envisioned a kingdom in which "the greatest among you must become like the youngest, and the leader like one who serves" (Luke 22:24-26). He offered his own example among them as "one who serves" rather than bullies, cajoles, or threatens (Luke 22:27). What we sometimes miss is that this was not a radical experiment he was offering. He was calling his disciples into the lifestyle he had experienced from eternity past with the Father and Holy Spirit.

Both in the earliest days of the church and in European-American civilization since the Enlightenment, the dominant cultural models for how people understand themselves in relationship to one another have crept into the church. The Roman Empire was a top-down structure of power, so the church of the Middle Ages functioned on that authoritarian model. The Enlightenment project for human life reacted to life under heavy-handed authority and held out autonomy as the ideal, so the call has been for self-determination based on the private interpretation of Scripture. Both models were wrong. Both tended to gravitate toward a doctrine of God as the Sovereign Individual—not a trinitarian (i.e., united-though-diverse) community but a unitarian (i.e., single-person) dominion—who imparts grace from the top down through the church's ordained hierarchy (in the Middle Ages) or epitomizes the independent deity who either created the world and stepped back to let it run (early-Enlightenment deism) or urges each human being to individualized spirituality through personal self-discovery (late-Enlightenment autonomy).

The church has a better model for its life and function. In the Trinity, the redeemed Bride of Christ finds both the individual and community existing harmoniously. The individual does not discover his identity within himself but in the exercise of self-giving within relationship. The church is a bride precisely because she exists in the context of mutual giving and receiving with Christ. He is not an abusive monarch. He is not an authoritarian corporation head. As a husband, he is anything but anxious to prove he is boss over his own house. To the contrary, "he nourishes and tenderly cares for [the church]…because we are members of his body" (Eph. 5:30).

One of the ways in which God the Son nourishes his bride is through our shared experience of worship. He becomes our link to the Godhead, the divine family; he invites us to participate in the triune life of God by means of the entrance he has provided through his self-giving act at Calvary. In worship, the risen Christ meets with us and in him we are transformed. We no longer simply know *about* God; we *know* him. He does not merely know *about* us and our creaturely needs; because of the Son, we have fellowship with the Father and Spirit, and God *knows* us.

Torrance offers this definition of worship informed by a trinitarian theology: "It is the gift of participating through the Spirit in the incarnate Son's communion with the Father."[10] He offers this definition as an alternative to human-centered worship that has people sitting in pews to watch the minister "doing his thing" and then exhorting us "to do our thing"—until we go home thinking we have done our duty until next week. He intends his definition to affirm that Christian worship finds its true focus in the priestly work of Christ on our behalf. Enabled by the indwelling Spirit of God, Christ enables our participation in the triune fellowship. He not only takes our moral failings and purifies them by his blood when we are converted but also takes our imperfect worship and, through the Spirit, enables us to draw near to God by participating in the perfect divine union.

## Our Worship Presenter

A central element of this idea about Jesus as priest has been obscured in our English translations of a text such as Hebrews 8:1-2. When the writer of Hebrews affirms that high priest Jesus is "a *minister* in the sanctuary and the true tent that the Lord, and not any mortal, has set up," more is being affirmed than Protestant readers are likely to hear from any English translation.

The original text calls Jesus the *leitourgos* of the heavenly sanctuary. The *leitourgos* is not an attendant or instructor. Neither is he the one who models what others should do. In that case, the writer might have called Jesus our *diakonos*. He is, instead, the "worship *leader*" or "worship *presenter*" in the throne room of

God. Perhaps we should wrestle with this idea for a while in light of the ongoing "worship wars" in the church of our time.

What is the right and best worship for us to offer our God? High-church liturgy? Low-church spontaneity? Middle-church eclecticism? Shall we use classical church music or praise choruses? What about drama? What about a thousand other things that have generated controversy? Which style of worship will generate God's pleasure with us and transform our hearts? *These are wrong-headed questions that reflect a wrong-headed view of worship.*

Humans are not the effective agents of worship, as if its effectiveness and power somehow arises from our use of proper techniques. In fact, we would dare suggest that *any* worship "style" is effective—once the nature of true worship is understood. And, as a corollary of that, some of our skirmishes along various fronts of the so-called "worship wars" surely stem from our abject failure to understand worship as the first-century author of the Hebrews material conceived it.

Against our Protestant rejection of the notion that a worship-leading priest has special access to God and does powerful things in worship that ordinary mortals cannot, the writer of Hebrews believes precisely that. Consistent with our Protestant rejection of the notion that a worship-leading *human* priest has special access to God and can perform rites the rest of us may not, he believes that Jesus alone is the effective agent of true worship. In the context of Hebrews, the high priestly worship of God the Son effectively sums up and brings to fulfillment the *leitourgia* (i.e., worship ritual) of Israel. His worship of God has replaced theirs. It is now the essence of Christian worship.

What makes worship meaningful and transformational for those who believe in Jesus is not our behaviors on Planet Earth but his ministrations in heaven on our behalf. The true and authentic worship Christians offer God is that which God has provided for us by his grace and which alone is acceptable to him. Take baptism as a case in point: Is baptism meaningful and transformational because of our understanding, administration, and reception of water? Of course not! The power of baptism is not in what we do but in what Christ has already done; our baptism in water is an event of participation in his death, burial, and resurrection. It is the invitation to imitate Jesus as he himself was announced as Son of God and empowered with the Spirit for ministry. It is our participation in the mystery and mission of God transforming us into the living body of Christ.

Or take another instance of Christian practice: Is the Lord's Supper meaningful and transformational because of our communion devotionals, silence or music during the meal, or choice of wine versus grape juice? Of course not! The power of the Lord's Supper is not in our methodology of approach to the event but lies in our mystical union with Christ and his body. Our eating and drinking of the communion meal is the sharing of remembrance, fellowship, encouragement, and hope based on his work. But it is much more! It is the intentional and conscious experience of Christ himself that cannot leave one untouched, unchanged. Transforming grace is mediated not through our meticulous, correct performance of the rite but through ministrations ongoing at the Father's right hand (cf. Rom. 5:10).

If you have followed this line of reasoning about baptism and the Lord's Supper, it should be easy now to grasp what Hebrews 8:1-2 says about worship generally. Are our praises, prayers, and proclamation meaningful and transformational because they are contemporary, spontaneous, and strewn with good illustrations? Or should our songs be traditional hymns, prayers prearranged and written, and sermons scholarly to a fault—without the fluff of stories and humor? That these have been our primary concerns about worship may explain why the worship wars happened at all. They betray the fact that we have missed the point of worship. Alas, we are inescapably people of culture and custom who are tossed about by taste and trends.

Just as baptism and the Lord's Supper initiate us into and connect us with Christ's own person, so does everything in worship. When we worship, it is what he does for us as high priest and *leitourgos* that causes anything to happen that is meaningful or transformational. Just as Christ is our wisdom and righteousness and redemption, so is he also our worship. We are admitted to them all by our faith in Jesus and not on the basis of our performance. On the basis of the atoning work of God the Son, God the Spirit makes our feeble attempts acceptable to God the Father. Through God the Son and by the renewing agency of God the Spirit, we receive back from God the Father made-whole versions of the broken lives we offer.

Perhaps our Protestant stress on the personal priesthood of every individual believer has made us lose sight of the work of Christ as high priest. We are not priests serving under contract to God—priests whose ability to get a positive response depends on what we do in events of worship. We are the covenant people of God who have been redeemed and who are being renewed and changed in Christ through the presence of the Holy Spirit within us. When we pray, preach, and praise, we are more correctly affirming the worship of our high priest than generating our own offerings to God.

> Therefore, anything we say about our worship—the forms of worship, its practice and procedure—must be said in the light of him to whom it is a response. It must be said in the light of the gospel of grace. We must ask ourselves whether our forms of worship convey the gospel. Are they an appropriate response to the gospel? Do they help people to apprehend the worship and ministry of Christ as he draws us by the Spirit into a life of shared communion, or do they hinder? Do they make the real presence of Christ transparent in worship, or do they obscure it? To answer these questions, we have to look at the meaning, the content of worship, before we can decide whether our traditions and procedures are adequate.[11]

### Worship as Surrender

Much of the modern discussion of worship is trite and misses the point. There can and should be different worship styles. There are, after all, different personalities, inclinations, and backgrounds among worshippers. So one church makes some deliberate choices for reasons specific to itself and its environment. Other congregations and whole denominations make different choices. We can discuss, encourage, or challenge these choices indefinitely and never get down to the central issue.

A church whose corporate worship is exactly the same as it was half a century ago may be smug and self-congratulatory against those who have made changes. Chances are, however, that arrogant judgments will more likely be passed by those who have changed some things in an effort to connect with people an older style of worship misses. Shame on both! The real significance of worship can be missed from either side of this judgmental divide.

So what *is* the nature of the worship God wants us to offer? How does one honor the ideal Jesus articulated about worship in Spirit/spirit and Truth/truth? How do we avail ourselves of the work of the Son of God as *leitourgos*?

Worship occurs when our desire for self-fulfillment gives way to self-surrender. When we are drawn into the trinitarian community of holiness, truth, and love, our penchant for enforcing legalistic rules for worship (i.e., worship is acceptable only when it includes this/these item/s and cannot include that/ those item/s) and our narcissistic individualism about worship (i.e., "*I* am giving God some of *my* worship and declaring him worthy of *my* affection!") give way to a focus on God.

> *When all Thy mercies,*
> *O my God,*
> *My rising soul surveys,*
> *Transported with the view,*
> *I'm lost*
> *In wonder, love, and praise.*
>
> —Joseph Addison

When authentic worship occurs, there are no "actors" or "performers" to be rated for their effectiveness. There are no pronouncements for ourselves or against others. Authentic homage is paid to the triune God when we enter a state of heart and life that

lifts us out of ourselves into what Paul labels "heavenly realms."
As in the rhythms of dancing, the self-forgetfulness of typing, or
the movement of a concert pianist's fingers across the keyboard,
one who has entered into the heart of a worship experience is
unlikely to be self-conscious about worship.

Worship is ultimately the yielding of ourselves in which we
perceive that we are not the center of the cosmos around which
all things revolve. To the contrary, God is. God alone, God
always, and God absolutely. That is why we pray, "*Your* kingdom come, *your* will be done on earth as it is in heaven" and
imitate the Incarnate Son by saying, "Not *my* will, but *yours* be
done." So we sing "All to Jesus, I surrender" or "O Lord, you're
beautiful." We may engage our bodies in a variety of ways—now
lifting hands, now bowing heads, now kneeling. We are alter-
nately moved to tears or laughter, applause or penitence.

Worship, when it is genuinely experienced, is not critiqued in
third-party mode; it is the mystery of being "lost in wonder, love,
and praise" in the communion between Creator and creature. Our
hearts have heard the divine invitation to enter the eternal community Father, Son, and Holy Spirit experience as One God; we
participate in that community. We offer our feeble adulation in
astonishment that our Holy God would allow such unworthy creatures into his presence, and Christ transforms our offering into his
perfect worship of the Father; the Spirit gives back an empowerment for living that enables us to present our bodies as living sacrifices to God in spiritual worship beyond the sanctuary.

## Conclusion

Worship of the triune God draws us out of the frenzied noise
of the world to hear the voice of God the Father, to review again
the faithful deeds of God the Son, and to receive renewal from
God the Holy Spirit. The very experience of worship is an invitation to participate in the perfect communion they share with
one another—and to model heavenly community among ourselves for all the world to see.

So enough of what Robert Webber calls "me-centered worship" that is all about "me" and "what I do in worship." Enough

of autonomous, independent human beings declaring God worthy of their worship. Instead, let us offer what we acknowledge as feeble, imperfect, and incomplete worship through the Incarnate Son who is the one true worship of God and thereby respond to his invitation into divine community. And let us take back from the experience lives renewed by divine power that could never again be open to the indictment of worshippers in Isaiah's time. People who have entered the community in which God reigns have been cleansed and set free from bondage to evil. That community seeks justice, rescues the oppressed, and defends the helpless. It radiates the joyful beauty of holiness for the whole world to see.

Worship is not merely *about* God. It is even more than *dialogue with God*. It is participation in his own triune interrelationship that enables us to know and be known by God. And in knowing God, we are saved and begin to experience life-in-community, self-emptying relationships, and life as it was meant to be lived.

### Notes

1. We struggle to find the term most appropriate to and least condescending toward those who do not confess faith in and love for Jesus Christ. More often than not, we will use "disciples" and "non-disciples" as our preferred terms. As in this sentence, however, we will sometimes use such common—but to us much less specific—terms as "unchurched" or "unbelieving." But some "believers" are hardly disciples! (cf. Jas. 2:19). And the goal we envision for "unchurched" persons is hardly articulated by saying we would like to see them "churched." What we do pray for both ourselves and others is that we would be true disciples of Christ Jesus—not only professing faith in but love for Jesus, not only living as good church members but as the kingdom people of God.

2. George R. Beasley-Murray, *Word Biblical Commentary: John* (Waco, TX: Word, 1987), p. 62.

3. Or, perhaps, "Spirit and Truth." The distinction in English between "spirit" and "Spirit" or "truth" and "Truth" cannot be settled by an appeal to the original-language text of John 4. Modern protocols for capitalization of

proper nouns are not observed in the Greek text of the New Testament. The oldest manuscripts available to us are written entirely in capital letters.

4. Cf. Gary M. Burge, *The Anointed Community* (Grand Rapids: Eerdmans, 1987), pp. 192-195.

5. See Deut. 33:7 and Psa. 33:20 where forms of this word refer to divine deliverance.

6. Stanley Grenz, "The Purpose of Sex: Toward a Theological Understanding of Human Sexuality," *Crux* 26, 2 (June 1990): 29-34.

7. While marriage is the fullest and deepest form of human community in Scripture, this is not to say that single, divorced, or widowed persons are somehow inferior as unmarried persons. It is not to claim that they are "incomplete" as to their personal worth outside marriage. The sexual dimension of every human life points to the need for connectedness with the human race and its Creator. There are ways of receiving others and giving of oneself that—while involving and acknowledging our sexual natures—are not outside the rules against fornication and adultery. Family, friendship, and a sense of belonging within a spiritual community are all important. In the New Testament, the community of the kingdom of God is elevated to a status above even that of marriage and family (cf. Mark 10:29-30). One who does not live in the context of physical union with a human partner may still experience the fullness of spiritual union with God through Christ as a part of his spiritual body, the church.

8. A recent book that has helped many begin to appreciate the significance of Trinitarian theology for worship is James B. Torrance, *Worship, Community & the Triune God of Grace* (Downers Grove: InterVarsity Press, 1996).

9. Stanley J. Grenz, *Theology for the Community of God* (Nashville: Broadman & Holman, 1994), p. 98.

10. Torrance, *Worship, Community & the Triune God of Grace*, p. 20.

11. Torrance, *Worship, Community & the Triune God of Grace*, p.15. The discussion of Christ as *leitourgos* and the implications of that for worship in the several paragraphs preceding this quotation are rooted in Torrance's discussion of the term.

Because the gospel the
church has to proclaim
concerns the announcement
of the fact and possibility
of renewed human
community in the love
of God, "the teaching of
the church" is, basically, the
church herself, as the sign
and the beginning of this
renewed community.
The verbal proclamation
of the message is merely
the articulation of the
community's self-
consciousness, of the
community's reality.

—Nicholas Lash

# 4. LOVE:
# THE RELATIONAL LINK

*You were dead through the trespasses and sins in which
you once lived, following the course of this world, following the ruler of the power of the air, the spirit that is now
at work among those who are disobedient. All of us once
lived among them in the passions of our flesh, following
the desires of flesh and senses, and we were by nature
children of wrath, like everyone else. But God, who is rich
in mercy, out of the great love with which he loved us
even when we were dead through our trespasses, made us
alive together with Christ—by grace you have been
saved—and raised us up with him and seated us with
him in the heavenly places in Christ Jesus, so that in the
ages to come he might show the immeasurable riches of
his grace in kindness toward us in Christ Jesus. For by
grace you have been saved through faith, and this is not
your own doing; it is the gift of God—not the result of
works, so that no one may boast. For we are what he has
made us, created in Christ Jesus for good works, which
God prepared beforehand to be our way of life.*

—Ephesians 2:1-10

"For by grace you have been saved." There aren't many more exciting words than those in all of Scripture for most of us. Christians across lines of race, gender, color, and language group share spiritual autobiographies that resonate with the reality that we were indeed dead through our life and lifestyle, and we recognized the need to be saved. Now we are saved from our sin, saved from the brokenness of our lives, saved from the pain and judgment and rejection that we might have received from others—especially those using guilt and coercion and works righteousness to tell us to earn our way to heaven. Grace: "God's unmerited favor," we say. Grace: the free gift of God— not the result of works lest we humans turn our salvation into bragging rights. Yet, there is some connection to works, good works, in this summary statement by Paul to the Ephesians. "We are what he made us, created in Christ Jesus for good works, which God prepared beforehand to be our way of life."

It is the last sentence that is most puzzling and difficult to comprehend in this text. Most of us have come to grips with earlier parts of the paragraph. We know—at least we think we comprehend—what it is like to be dead in sin, to know the weight of personal spiritual failure hanging as a millstone around one's neck. We know what it is like to follow the desires of flesh and senses, to buy into the messages constantly thrown at us that tell us our value in this life comes from physical appearance, comes from our collection of stuff, comes from our political system, comes from our cultural superiority to the rest of the world. We know what it is like to discover that the cultural icons that offer us security, identity, and personal value are shallow and empty promises. The right house and car and make-up and toothpaste and designer label can't make me an athlete or a better mate or a better person. We know what it is like to be dead in sin.

We know the exhilaration that came from discovering that we could stop trying to merit God's favor. One doesn't have to have all the answers to Bible trivia in order to be saved. We don't have to have perfect attendance. We don't "have to" anything. So we love to read the stories which have Jesus revealing God's unmerited favor to undeserving souls. One of them is about a woman caught in adultery in John 8. "Let him who is without sin cast the first stone," Jesus said. That stopped those judgmental types dead in their tracks. "Go your way, and from now on do not sin again," Jesus told the woman. Or the story of the rich tax collector Zacchaeus. Or the Samaritan woman at Jacob's well. Or the "lady of the evening" who came and washed the feet of Jesus and made the Pharisee, Simon, look like the ungrateful, self-righteous hypocrite he was.

### What Comes Next?

Have you ever wondered what happened next in those stories? Did the woman leave the presence of Jesus and abandon her adulterous past? Did Zacchaeus give his money away and then find a job other than collecting taxes? Did the Samaritan woman get married and live happily ever after? Or did the boyfriend dump her when she decided to follow Jesus? Did the "lady of the evening" find a way out of the sex trade after Jesus announced that her faith had saved her and made her whole?

That's the sticky part of Paul's words to the Ephesians. Those who have been saved by grace through faith, not by works lest any of us should boast, have been created in Christ Jesus "for good works." Similar to the words of Paul in Galatians 6 and 2 Corinthians 5, this seems to be new-creation language for Paul. We are created *in Christ Jesus*—that is our new-creation identity. But then comes the rest of the story.

In Christ Jesus, God gives us a new way of life. But that new way for living is actually the existence that he had in mind for us in the beginning. Now that we are becoming whole humans again, the life we were originally designed to live becomes a very real option—for the first time in our experience. But what does the new life of a redeemed personality look like? When do people get that part right? Most of Paul's letters seem to address the people in Christ who haven't gotten it right yet. They had been filled with the Spirit in Corinth and Ephesus and Galatia and Thessalonica and Philippi and Rome and Colossae, but the rest of the story was still a work in progress. And we don't know

the outcomes! What we do know is that the life of faith empowered by this gracious activity of Jesus is not freedom from hard-
ship or failure or suffering.

It doesn't get any easier when we leave Paul and the epistles
behind and return to the teachings and actions of Jesus. Jesus'
own words aren't simple to practice either. Think for a moment
about the so-called Sermon on the Plain of Luke 6, when Jesus
tells his hearers that following him means loving one's enemies
and doing good to those who mistreat us. Where is the language
of grace in this call to love in tough circumstances?

> But I say to you that listen, Love your enemies, do
> good to those who hate you, bless those who curse you,
> pray for those who abuse you. If anyone strikes you on
> the cheek, offer the other also; and from anyone who
> takes away your coat do not withhold even your shirt.
> Give to everyone who begs from you; and if anyone
> takes away your goods, do not ask for them again. Do
> to others as you would have them do to you. If you love
> those who love you, what credit is that to you? For even
> sinners love those who love them. If you do good to
> those who do good to you, what credit is that to you? For
> even sinners do the same. If you lend to those from
> whom you hope to receive, what credit is that to you?
> Even sinners lend to sinners, to receive as much again.
> But love your enemies, do good, and lend, expecting
> nothing in return. Your reward will be great, and you will
> be children of the Most High; for he is kind to the
> ungrateful and the wicked. Be merciful, just as your
> Father is merciful (Luke 6:27-36).

Jesus goes on to speak of not judging others and the power
of forgiveness, but he also talks about good trees bearing good
fruit and bad trees bearing bad fruit. He concludes with a strong
saying about keeping and doing his words:

> Why do you call me "Lord, Lord," and do not do
> what I tell you? I will show you what someone is like

who comes to me, hears my words, and acts on them. That one is like a man building a house, who dug deeply and laid the foundation on rock; when a flood arose, the river burst against that house but could not shake it, because it had been well built. But the one who hears and does not act is like a man who built a house on the ground without a foundation. When the river burst against it, immediately it fell, and great was the ruin of that house (Luke 6:46-49).

There is a strong juxtaposition in Jesus' teaching that puts his compassion and mercy alongside strong demands of accountability and practice. Again, it would be easy simply to say that we are to be merciful to others while being doers of the word ourselves. We believe that much is true, but we also have experienced the need to be merciful to ourselves more than a few times. In our ministries, we have also observed that churches can get caught up in the same dilemma in their communal experience. So how are we to know what time it is? When does love act mercifully and when does tough love demand accountability? How do we live together in ways that reflect both the accountability of Jesus and his compassion and mercy toward the sinner?

"I'm not going to that church anymore," Mike declared. "They are so rigid and so self-righteous! They think you have to be perfect and follow every one of their rules or you just don't fit. But the truth is, they're just a bunch of hypocrites. They're just like the Pharisees—worried about every minor infraction of their precious rules, but they don't really seem to care about anybody but themselves. You have to think exactly like they do or you're not a Christian. And they're all a bunch of sour-pusses! You hardly ever see them crack a smile in church—or anywhere else for that matter."

"I'm not going to that church anymore," said Susan. "They don't stand for anything! They talk about love and grace all the time, but what they really mean is you can sin whenever and however you want because we're all sinners anyway. Forgiveness is so cheap at that church that you have to wonder what's the point in going in the first place? Where's the accountability? They tolerate every sin and every sinner. They might as well hang out a sign that says, 'Come to our church—no repentance necessary!'"

> *I give you a new commandment, that you love one another. Just as I have loved you, you also should love one another. By this will everyone know that you are my disciples, if you have love for one another.*
>
> —John 13:34-35

I'm not going to that church anymore, they don't worship right. They allow this. They don't allow that. They do or don't. They can't or won't. There is no end to the indictments people bring against us.

So what happened to love and mercy and not passing judgment—or does this thinking happen because of the need for accountability and practicing righteousness? Somehow in our world we seem to have developed two extreme ways of approaching this business of being Christian and being the church. One side is very concerned that God's standards of righteousness be observed; the other is concerned that—in the name of love—tolerance should be the watchword. Both groups have Scripture to support them. So which is right?

Then, what happens when we overlay the cultural surroundings on our efforts to be the church? It is not possible for us to leave these texts in a biblical vacuum. We have to read them in the midst of our culture and in light of the other influences that define our sense of personhood and identity.

### Life in a Consumer Culture

Appearance, affluence, achievement—one writer calls them "the three A's of conventional wisdom" in our culture.[1] They are the means by which we measure our own worth and that of other people in American society. Conventional wisdom says it is our outward appearance that gives us our principal identity. Certain body types, certain fashions of clothing, certain colors of skin—these superficial things not only identify us as individuals but stereotype us with those who share common appearance features. Enormous amounts of effort, energy, and income are spent on reshaping or making over our physical appearance so we can be seen in ways we deem most appropriate to our culture. Even when good health and long life are the goals of our fitness routines and eating habits, we are never far from a keen interest in how we look—too old or too young, too thin or too fat, too much hair or not enough. Conventional wisdom says that how one looks on the outside tells us what we should think about ourselves and what others will think about us.

Then comes affluence. It is the goal of good living in our society. Those who are successful can be recognized by their accumulation of things. Tied closely to anyone's definition of the American dream is the accumulation of wealth—whether one is born into it or educated into it or gifted to it athletically or by sheer hard work and ingenuity earns it or by the chance selection of six lucky numbers wins the lottery. There are winners and losers in life, and conventional wisdom says that you can always identify the winners by their affluence. Reality TV is the new game show approach to affluence, isn't it? Sing or dance or date or survive your way to a million dollars. Obviously appearance plays a huge role in most efforts to win the prize. There are certain body types that likely won't make it to the screening room. But for those who do, if you can win the big prize, then what? Celebrity status?

That leads to the third A of conventional wisdom—achievement. We gain identity and place and power and self-understanding through accomplishment in our culture. We reward academic achievement in the world of education. We determine status and power in almost any other part of our culture by assigning achievement goals and standards. If you want to become something you are not in this world, you are thrust immediately into the world of competition to achieve. But this third A is always connected to the first two. Achievement is what we are doing as the means to obtain the affluence and appearance we covet. Conventional wisdom says that we all have the "potential" to achieve our financial goals. We pursue the highest levels of education or training or management skills or work on our physical appearance in order to achieve. It all becomes a vicious cycle. And we find ourselves along for the ride.

At the root of all three of these icons of conventional wisdom are comparison and value judgment with regard to self and other people. Appearance always differentiates between people, always creates haves and have-nots, often makes assumptions about the value of life itself. Affluence is identified with success and immediately identifies failure as well. And we all know who the under-achievers are. We know who isn't living up to his or her potential. There are those who achieve life's weighty goals—and there are those who don't. Appearance, affluence, and achievement set the standards by which we judge and are judged. Perhaps even more dangerous than the judgment of others and the self-judgment that occurs is the temptation to take shortcuts to achieve our goals of appearance and affluence.

So we come to church to escape all of that! After all, we understand that the foolishness of God is wiser that the wisdom of the world. But what happens when the ways of the world get brought into the church building? What happens when appearance and achievement and affluence actually become criteria for church fellowship? What happens when power and control and privilege are asserted and there is a clash of wills? What happens when we then start proof-texting each other? In other words, what happens when status within the institutional church replaces inclusion within the relational body of Christ? And would you be surprised to learn that Mike and Susan who were quoted earlier actually attend the same church?

Where do you suppose God's will is to be found in the stories of Susan and Mike? Jesus said, "Be perfect as your heavenly father is perfect." He also said, "Be merciful as your heavenly father is merciful." "Bear fruit that befits your repentance," Jesus taught. "Judge not, lest you be judged," Jesus said. What about the Parable of the Prodigal Son? It affirms that Jesus loves sinners and tax collectors. Yes, but what about the Parable of the Wise and Foolish Builders? What about the Pharisee and the tax collector? Yes, but then what about the demand that our righteousness exceed that of the Pharisees and scribes?

> For the message about the cross is foolishness to those who are perishing, but to us who are being saved it is the power of God. For it is written, "I will destroy the wisdom of the wise, and the discernment of the discerning I will thwart." Where is the one who is wise? Where is the scribe? Where is the debater of this age? Has not God made foolish the wisdom of the world? For since, in the wisdom of God, the world did not know God through wisdom, God decided, through the foolishness of our proclamation, to save those who believe. For Jews demand signs and Greeks desire wisdom, but we proclaim Christ crucified, a stumbling block to Jews and foolishness to Gentiles, but to those who are the called, both Jews and Greeks, Christ the power of God and the wisdom of God. For God's foolishness is wiser than human wisdom, and God's weakness is stronger than human strength (1 Cor. 1:18-25).

The foolishness of the cross rests precisely in the paradoxical understandings and relationships that our faith claims press upon us. In order to live, we must die. In order to do the works of God, we must stop our performances. In order to experience full fellowship with one another, we must give up self-selecting preferences. In order to experience God's wisdom, we must admit our own foolishness. In order to become one in the Spirit, we must give back to God our individuated church identities—while understanding that each church is a microcosm of the whole.

## Grace: The Rest of the Story

In her book *Amazing Grace*, Kathleen Norris writes a series of meditations on the Christian faith. The subtitle of the book is

*A Vocabulary of Faith.*[2] Throughout the book she writes about the language of faith, the words that become the "insider" language by which we Christians live. There are sections on salvation and redemption, incarnation and prayer, faith and preaching, righteousness and truth. There are also sections on eschatology, exorcism, inquisition, apostasy, and ecstasy. In each case, she writes three or four pages, usually reflecting on her personal experience of the word, or perhaps telling someone else's story. Sometimes she uses Bible stories to illustrate the meaning of the term. Near the middle there is a meditation on the word that gives the book its title—grace. Her method of handling it was both surprising and brilliant. Having read some of her other works, you might have expected her to reflect on her own journey of faith. She was raised in church, but soured on both God and church on account of her church experiences. A couple of decades later, she found herself being drawn back into relationship with both.

She picked a story from the Bible. But her choice was surprising. It is not even a New Testament story—the conversion of Saul or Peter or one of those stories in the Gospels. Her story to illustrate the meaning of the word grace is the story of Jacob when he was fleeing for his life from his brother Esau. Jacob, the supplanter, was the twin son of Isaac and Rebekah to whom his mother showed favoritism. Jacob is the one who saw his hungry brother in a vulnerable situation and schemed to cheat him out of his birthright. He was the one who lied to his blind father in order to steal the blessing of the firstborn. Now Jacob is the one alone at night in the middle of nowhere, headed to live with relatives he has never met—assuming he does not get killed along the way. And he has this dream.

> Jacob left Beer-sheba and went toward Haran. He came to a certain place and stayed there for the night, because the sun had set. Taking one of the stones of the place, he put it under his head and lay down in that place. And he dreamed that there was a ladder set up on the earth, the top of it reaching to heaven; and the angels of God were ascending and descending on it.

And the LORD stood beside him and said, "I am the LORD, the God of Abraham your father and the God of Isaac; the land on which you lie I will give to you and to your offspring; and your offspring shall be like the dust of the earth, and you shall spread abroad to the west and to the east and to the north and to the south; and all the families of the earth shall be blessed in you and in your offspring. Know that I am with you and will keep you wherever you go, and will bring you back to this land; for I will not leave you until I have done what I have promised you." Then Jacob woke from his sleep and said, "Surely the LORD is in this place—and I did not know it!" And he was afraid, and said, "How awesome is this place! This is none other than the house of God, and this is the gate of heaven" (Gen. 28:10-17).

Don't miss his surprise when he wakes up! "Surely the LORD is in this place—and I did not know it!" There had been nothing in Jacob's attitude or actions to this point to suggest he has ever given much thought to the presence of the LORD any place. If you needed a poster-boy for someone who made life impossi ble for others, who destroyed every relationship he had to this point, and who was now adrift because of his deceitful behaviors, Jacob would be your guy. Yet the heavens are opened to him, and the LORD showers him with promise and blessing. "The LORD stood beside him and said...."

What should Jacob do with this amazing grace? He decides to build an altar and worship and call the place Bethel, the "house of God." Then comes a startling response: Jacob makes a vow, saying, "If God will be with me, and will keep me in this way that I go, and will give me bread to eat and clothing to wear, so that I come again to my father's house in peace, then the LORD shall be my God, and this stone, which I have set up for a pillar, shall be God's house; and of all that you give me I will surely give one-tenth to you" (Genesis 28:20-22). Having received the unmerited favor of God, the free gift of promise and steadfast love from the creator of the universe, Jacob says, "If you really keep this up, God, and deliver on your promises, I'll give you ten percent!"

What's so amazing about the story of Jacob is that we have no idea whether he delivers on the vow or not! We do know that his life of deception was far from finished. Having experienced the power and promise of God did not mean that Jacob suddenly experiences only the joy of salvation. Duplicity and deceit will continue to be his way of life when he reaches the home of his uncle Laban. He will end up with Leah when he really just wanted Rachel. His unequal treatment of his two wives will lead to jealousy and deceit that combine to make his life miserable. He will end up with children from four different women, and the children will get along about as well as he did with his own brother. He will grow wealthy while serving his uncle, but only through a series of deceptions by both him and his uncle. Yet, somehow, when he is making the journey back home and is scared to death that his brother Esau is now going to kill him, he will have another divine encounter.

Again he finds himself alone in the middle of the night. This time a mysterious stranger appears, and the trickster and the new arrival wrestle all through the night—with neither of them being able to prevail.

> When the man saw that he did not prevail against Jacob, he struck him on the hip socket; and Jacob's hip was put out of joint as he wrestled with him. Then he said, "Let me go, for the day is breaking." But Jacob said, "I will not let you go, unless you bless me." So he said to him, "What is your name?" And he said, "Jacob." Then the man said, "You shall no longer be called Jacob, but Israel, for you have striven with God and with humans, and have prevailed." Then Jacob asked him, "Please tell me your name." But he said, "Why is it that you ask my name?" And there he blessed him (Gen. 32:25-29).

Even at the end, Jacob is still trying to gain control by being able to name this mysterious presence. He simply receives the blessing instead.

Perhaps Kathleen Norris chose the story of Jacob's dream to illustrate God's amazing grace because we know the rest of the story. We know much more about the faith failures of Jacob than we know of his faith successes. We don't know if he actually gave God ten percent of anything. We do know that God's promise of presence and blessing sustained Jacob in the midst of horrible, hateful events in his life. In a person that we otherwise would never suspect, God's brings about his wonderful work of transformation.

We love the story because it suggests that God's unmerited favor, God's grace, isn't conditioned by the stuttering, on-again-off-again performance of its recipients. But we also want to respect what is different about God's grace as it has now been mediated to us humans in Christ. We no longer live as Jacob did, with unpredicted and unpredictable appearances of Yahweh affirming his love and presence with us when we least expect it. Jacob had the promise of God-presence in his dream, but he had no other person who shared that moment or that vision. In Christ, the promise of God-presence comes to us in light, not darkness; it comes in community, not in isolation. In Christ, more than a dream is given to bolster faith. We are given each other and the testimony of each other's stories. In Christ, God promises to indwell us and empower us for these good works that he prepared beforehand. In Christ, God gives us a way of life and surrounds us with other new-creation people who are on the faith journey with us.

> *Grace is love that crosses and stoops and rescues.*
>
> —John Stott

But there is one part of the Jacob story that does still factor into our own stories, it would seem. God made his most startling announcements of presence and promise to Jacob in two of the darkest moments of his life. But Jacob does not have a vision of God every time he has a horribly dark event in his life. The death of Rachel and the apparent death of his beloved son Joseph bring no immediate word from the LORD. God is not absent from the journey, however, just because Jacob has no dream or personal encounter. He is still present, still fulfilling the work that he prepared beforehand—even when Jacob is unaware.

The reality of God's grace in our lives is that God's unmerited favor is always at work in us, whether we feel it at the moment or not. It is the empowering presence that moment by moment both makes us accountable for our actions and empowers Christ-like performance. His creative works most often come to us through the relationships that we consider most important but in which we mess up most often. It is in the steadfast love of our spouses and children that we continually discover afresh what unmerited favor means. It is in the painfully slow journey toward being a better husband/wife, mom/dad, son/daughter that we catch glimpses of transformation—the grace of God's new-creation work forging the life that God intended for all who have been created in his image. That same journey of transformation runs through all of our relationships—from the most obvious and important to the least. In fact, God often uses the stranger to produce the greatest changes in our direction.

### Grace in Community: Love

Grace and renewal, transformation and accountability, security in relationship to God, authentic community in relationship with one another—the inevitable outcome of all these things is *love*. And why is such an outcome "inevitable"? Because the authentic presence of God in the life of either an individual believer or a community of his children will be revealed in the reflection of God's essence. And God is love.

In a short sermon-epistle that may well have accompanied the Gospel of John when it was originally circulated, the now-elderly apostle was concerned to put Christians of the late first century on their guard against doctrinal heresy. Some secessionist false teachers had reinterpreted Jesus through the lenses of their commitment to a strain of Greek philosophy that had them denying the Incarnation—and thus the atoning work of the Son of God. For example, people such as the apostle's contemporary

Cerinthus would confess Jesus to be a wise, pious, but otherwise ordinary mortal on whom a distant divine emanation (i.e., Christ) descended for a brief time. He would not, however, confess him as God in the flesh. And the failure of such people to honor Jesus of Nazareth as God come in human form to redeem us from sin made them false teachers. Instead of speaking the message God had given, they recast it in terms of the world's self-seeking quest for appearance, affluence, and achievement in order to get and hold a following. Thus John wrote:

> Beloved, do not believe every spirit, but test the spirits to see whether they are from God; for many false prophets have gone out into the world. By this you know the Spirit of God: every spirit that confesses that Jesus Christ has come in the flesh is from God, and every spirit that does not confess Jesus is not from God. And this is the spirit of the antichrist, of which you have heard that it is coming; and now it is already in the world. Little children, you are from God, and have conquered them; for the one who is in you is greater than the one who is in the world. They are from the world; therefore what they say is from the world, and the world listens to them. We are from God. Whoever knows God listens to us, and whoever is not from God does not listen to us. From this we know the spirit of truth and the spirit of error (1 John 4:1-6; cf. 2:22-23; 2 John 7).

Interestingly, though, John also gave a second test by which Christian faith was (and is) to be tested in the church. John saw the false teachers of his time and place exposed not only by their deficient confession (i.e., "every spirit that does not confess Jesus is not from God," 1 John 4:3) but by their unloving behaviors. At 4:7 he picks up the theme introduced at 3:10: "The children of God and the children of the devil are revealed in this way: all who do not do what is right are not from God, nor are those who do not love their brothers and sisters."

For John, the life of a local church as a holy community in which the love of God is made real to all its members is essential

to Christian orthodoxy. So, while the false teachers created a following made up of people attracted to the world's preoccupation with its selfish concerns, John appealed for those who loved
the truth to embrace the lifestyle that would confirm its presence
in their hearts. In this section, however, he goes beyond what
has been written already at 1 John 3:10-24. What he presented
there as the divine commandment to love is now traced to its origin in God. He claims that people who have been born of God
are the only ones who can really understand the nature of self-
giving love. Only because we have seen it modeled perfectly in
Christ can we embrace it for ourselves, and only because the
Holy Spirit lives in us can we be empowered to love as Jesus did.

> Beloved, let us love one another, because love is from
> God; everyone who loves is born of God and knows
> God. Whoever does not love does not know God, for
> God is love. God's love was revealed among us in this
> way: God sent his only Son into the world so that we
> might live through him. In this is love, not that we loved
> God but that he loved us and sent his Son to be the
> atoning sacrifice for our sins. Beloved, since God loved
> us so much, we also ought to love one another. No one
> has ever seen God; if we love one another, God lives in
> us, and his love is perfected in us (1 John 4:7-12).

The affirmation "love is from God" could be translated "love
is *out of* God" or paraphrased "love *originates in and flows from*
God." That is, love is to God as light is to the sun of our solar
system. John himself has introduced the light metaphor for God
at 1:5 when he wrote: "God is light and in him there is no darkness at all." Darkness doesn't originate with God. Sin does not
have its origin in him. Neglect, abuse, and hatred are not part of
his nature. God can only act in ways that are consistent with his
nature, and God's nature is love. So a community that does not
live in, affirm, and share love does not belong to him. "Whoever
does not love does not know God, for God is love" (1 John 4:8).
    You've been told before that there are multiple words in the

Greek language to express various dimensions of the sentiment we call love. In an old commentary on John's letters, Neil Alexander reviewed the fundamental distinction among three of those words in a helpful way. *Eros* is acquisitive love; it is the desire to possess and use—perhaps the desire for sex, money, truth, or power. *Philia* is the love of sisterhood and brotherhood; it is used of friendship that tends to be mutually beneficial and mutually satisfying. *Agape* is not so much an emotion of attraction, desire, or calculation of mutual benefit as it is an act of the will; it is a conscious decision to do what is in another's best interest. Alexander summarized his explanation this way: *eros* is all take, *philia* is give and take, *agape* is all give.[3]

God alone has pure, self-giving love as the essence of his nature. This sort of love, whenever and wherever practiced, has its origin with God. His image and likeness are stamped on the human heart, and we occasionally see someone act with what we call altruism or true unselfishness—a rescue worker rushing toward the Twin Towers on 9/11 rather than fleeing. That spirit is within the human heart because we are created with the capacity to reflect his nature as our creator. But the only one who can act in that spirit of self-giving constantly and without exception is God himself. As an event, that love was exhibited in the advent, life, and atoning death of Jesus Christ (1 John 4:9-10); as a process, it is to be carried from generation to generation through Christ's people (1 John 4:11-12).

Many people have experienced "love" only as someone else's desire to possess and use them; they have been manipulated, hurt, and abandoned in the name of love. Others know "love" only in the sense of bartering; they have been taught to

> *It is not a matter of thinking a great deal but of loving a great deal, so do whatever arouses you most to love.*
>
> —Mother Teresa

give of themselves only when they can be sure of getting something back. And these wounded, jaded, sad people make up the vast majority of the population of our world. The church is supposed to be an alternative community of holy living in which people love one another as God has loved them. When that goal is achieved, "God lives in us, and his love is perfected in us" (4:12b). To say that God's love is perfected in us simply means that the love Christians learn to show one another in community is really God's own love flowing through us. And that community becomes a proof to the world that God's love is real. People who did not experience care, nurture, and protection in other communities (i.e., family, neighborhood, school) are supposed to discover it in this community (i.e., the church).

What a shame that churches have too often preached the gospel not as love and grace but as fear and guilt. "If you died tonight, would you go to hell?" "Is sex with someone who is not your husband worth the fires of hell?" "Don't you know that alcoholics and drug addicts are destined for hell?"

*Do you really think the best way to call people to Christ is by preaching the fear of hell?* To the contrary, John believed and taught that the love of God is more powerful as a motivation to righteousness than the fear of hell.

> By this we know that we abide in him and he in us, because he has given us of his Spirit. And we have seen and do testify that the Father has sent his Son as the Savior of the world. God abides in those who confess that Jesus is the Son of God, and they abide in God. So we have known and believe the love that God has for us.
>
> God is love, and those who abide in love abide in God, and God abides in them. Love has been perfected among us in this: that we may have boldness on the day of judgment, because as he is, so are we in this world. There is no fear in love, but perfect love casts out fear; for fear has to do with punishment, and whoever fears has not reached perfection in love. We love because he first loved us. Those who say, "I love God," and hate

their brothers or sisters, are liars; for those who do not love a brother or sister whom they have seen, cannot love God whom they have not seen. The commandment we have from him is this: those who love God must love their brothers and sisters also (1 John 4:13-21).

The fundamental message of the gospel is not that Christ saves from hell but that he embodies the Father's love in giving us new life. The *driving force for new life* in Christ is not the fear of hell but the empowering presence of the Holy Spirit. And the *sustaining power for faithfulness* until Christ's return is not the fear of judgment but the assurance and boldness that result from living in a supportive community of authentic Christian love.

Maybe that is the problem with the spiritual life of some of us. We have not heard, been educated in, and had modeled for us the gospel as grace. We know it better as guilt and shame. We experience it as judgment. We receive it as rescue from hell. So we build churches that are more institutional than relational. But, no! The gospel is the message that love has become a baby at Bethlehem, God has become defenseless before evil, and the atonement has been secured by his self-giving at the cross. Thus we can live in holy community with one another and imitate the love we have experienced from God in the ways we care for one another.

But is that the common experience of church? Is this the way church is presented—or should we say "caricatured"—in the media? Why, if it were, people would be knocking down our doors to be part of the experience. Church would be a slice of heaven on earth that everyone would want to taste.

### God's Place of Belonging

Created as we were for relationship, it ought not surprise us to find that the disconnected lives most people live are unfulfilling and even unhealthy. Oh, we go to work along crowded highways and streets, work in sight of others, and sit in packed church buildings. But most of our relationships don't have much quality to them. There is no real depth or warmth. There are lots of acquaintances but few friendships. And it is painful to have no one with whom to share your innermost self and your most private feelings, your severest heartaches and greatest joys.

Research done at the University of Michigan just before the end of the twentieth century studied just under 3,000 men and women in the United States, Finland, and Sweden. It concluded that a lack of social relationships heightens one's susceptibility to illness and death. The researchers claimed that loneliness is as significant to mortality rates as smoking, high blood pressure, high cholesterol, and obesity. The sort of isolation focused on in that study was characterized by having nobody with whom to share one's private feelings, hopes, and fears. The lead researchers estimated that fully ten to twenty percent of people have close contact with others less than once a week. That percentage has probably grown rather than declined since their research was published. The same study showed that men are more devastated by loneliness than women—probably, researchers theorized, because women tend to create a higher quality of relationship than men.

> *It is impossible to love Christ without loving others in proportion as these others are moving towards Christ. And it is impossible to love others in a spirit of broad human communion without moving nearer to Christ.*
>
> —Pierre Teilhard de Chardin

Plato envisioned an ideal state in his *Republic,* and Sir Thomas More wrote of an ideal society he named *Utopia.* In the New Testament, God's place of belonging is called *ekklesia* and the relationship among its members is *koinonia.* Yet we hesitate to translate the former "church" and the latter "fellowship" for the simple reason that we have cheapened these English terms to mean an innocuous Sunday gathering and pot-luck dinner or my group and its criteria for membership.

In its purest and best instances, the church exists in the world now as an outpost of the kingdom of God. The church is not the fully realized kingdom of heaven, but it is an inbreaking of that kingdom and is a group of its citizens in process of spiritual formation. Its presence in the world bears witness to the cross and makes it a microcosm of God's kingdom. It testifies to a view of reality that takes eternity more seriously than time. As a visible community of faith, it senses the call of God to bear witness to life in the midst of death, truth in the midst of lies, joy in the midst of despair, and good in the midst of evil.

Against the hellish isolation of our time, the church must be a group of people in congregation (lit, gathered-togetherness). The *ekklesia* of Christ has not only been called out of the world but has been called together for his purposes. This doesn't mean that we are always together in large groups but that we are always together in spirit. Each of us must take the risk to relate to others who share the view of the cross, eternity, and virtue that we profess. Against a cultural reluctance to make commitments, we have committed to be God's presence for one another.

So we assemble on the Lord's Day, celebrate our call from God, discern the body of Christ at the table with our fellow-believers, and affirm one another. When we do so, we must allow the Spirit of God to quicken us by his presence, to renew holy zeal in our hearts. But beyond our times of spiritual renewal *en masse*, we must be willing to seek and be open to experience contact with one another that allows spiritual intimacy. These are burden-bearing, joy-disclosing, service-sharing experiences that cannot happen in whole-church assemblies. They are too personal. They require small-group and one-on-one settings in which men and women abandon defensiveness and lies in order to become vulnerable to one another. We open our hearts without condemnation from the rest of the group. With the pain of self-judgment already so intense it can hardly be tolerated, we bare our insecurities, addictions, infidelities, and failures to one another as the beginning point for recovery. Without fear of envy in such a community, we celebrate our triumphs, good fortune, temptations resisted, and successes. There is a healing mix of tears and laughter and applause as people who are included in the Bride of Christ recognize themselves in one another—and celebrate the Bridegroom's love.

Where can that ever-growing ten to twenty percent of lonely people come out of isolation into community? Where does a quarrelsome person learn to lighten up? Where does the guilt-laden soul come to terms with what is locked away in the deepest part of her heart? Where does someone who has been betrayed and driven even deeper underground find a place that is safe enough to risk trusting again? Is there a place where we can weep with those who weep and rejoice with those who rejoice—without sensing either reproach or resentment? Is there a place where sinners can be loved and accepted—without being coddled, tolerated for self-destructive behaviors, and allowed to infect the group with evil? Is there a place where the weak can be supported and carried—without being reduced to unhealthy dependence?

God the Father created such a relational community through the life, death, and resurrection of God the Son and sustains it even today by the presence of the God the Holy Spirit. It is variously called the Body of Christ, the Family of God, the Church of the Firstborn Ones, or the Bride of Christ. It is the Community of Faith for male and female, black and white, Jew and Gentile, drunk and teetotaler, employed and unemployed, single and married, rich and poor—anyone who seeks divine love and meaning, support and empowerment. Here we share our stories and discover ourselves in one another—and God at work in us all.

The thing that makes the church into a true spiritual community rather than a mere religious institution is the deliberate act of submitting all things to the conscious presence of God and his holy will. Golf tournaments, child-care classes, financial management courses, softball teams, and the like are neither inappropriate to an authentically Christian lifestyle nor improper offerings for a church. But it is not simply that we are sharing social events with other Christians that creates *koinonia* (i.e., fellowship, community) and nurtures spiritual health and maturity. It is a determined focus on Jesus and quest for the powerful presence of the Holy Spirit that makes all these events in relationship spiritual, healthy, and redemptive. Education, counseling, business, marriage—not one of these things is "Christian" simply because the persons doing them are church members. It is focus on the reign of God in all these relationships that makes them truly and distinctively Christian. And love is the relational link that ties us together as a community of faith.

The late Henri Nouwen taught at Notre Dame, Yale, and Harvard. But he chose to spend the last ten years of his life, from 1986 to 1996, at the L'Arche Daybreak community in Toronto in order to minister among people with mental and physical disabilities. He tells the story of one man that is particularly moving as a testimony to the need we all have for the church as fellowship and community, a place for making our lives visible to one another in the light of God's healing grace.

A *Life Story Book* is a collection of photographs, stories, and letters put together as a sort of biography. When Bill came to Daybreak as a sixteen-year-old, he brought few memories with him. He had had a very troublesome childhood and hardly any consistent experiences of love and friendship. His past was so broken, so painful, and so lonely that he had chosen to forget it. He was a man without a history.

But during twenty-five years at Daybreak, he gradually has become a different person. He has made friends. He has developed a close relationship with a family he can visit on weekends or holidays, joined a bowling club, learned woodworking, and traveled with me to places far and wide. Over the years he has created a life worth remembering. He even found the freedom and courage to recall some of his painful childhood experiences and to reclaim his deceased parents as people who had given him life and love notwithstanding their limitations....

Many came together for the occasion [of celebrating Bill's *Life Story Book*]. Bill held the book and lifted it up

for all to see. It was a beautifully colored ring binder
with many artistically decorated pages. Although it was
Bill's book, it was the work of many people.

Then we blessed the book and Bill, who held it. I
prayed that this book might help Bill let many people
know what a beautiful man he is and what a good life
he was living. I also prayed
that Bill would remember all
the moments of his life—his
joys as well as his sorrows—
with a grateful heart.

> *Indifference, not
> hate, is the strongest
> enemy of love.*
>
> —C.S. Lewis

While I prayed tears started
to flow from Bill's eyes. When
I finished he threw his arms
around me and cried loudly.
His tears fell on my shoulder
while everyone in the circle
looked at us with a deep understanding of what was
happening. Bill's life had been lifted up for all to see, and
he had been able to say it was a life to be grateful for....

The cup of sorrow and joy, when lifted for others to
see and celebrate, becomes a cup to life. It is so easy for
us to live truncated lives because of hard things that have
happened in our past, which we prefer not to remember.
Often the burdens of our past seem too heavy for us to
carry alone. Shame and guilt make us hide part of ourselves and thus make us live half lives.

We truly need each other to claim all of our lives and
to live them to the fullest. We need each other to move
beyond our guilt and shame and to become grateful, not
just for our successes and accomplishments but also for
our failures and shortcomings. We need to be able to let
our tears flow freely, tears of sorrow as well as tears of
joy, tears that are as rain on dry ground. As we thus lift
our lives for each other, we can truly say: *To Life*,
because all we have lived now becomes the fertile soil
for the future.[4]

## Conclusion

To live in love as God's redeemed community is to live out Paul's words to the Corinthians that we quote so often at weddings and too little in community settings. They are words of the heart, words that reflect not just the behavior of two individuals in a marriage but of God's kingdom community in the world. It is time to hear them as a test of our orthodoxy and faithfulness to Christ. And it is time to stop excusing ourselves from their practical demands.

> Love never gives up.
> Love cares more for others than for self.
> Love doesn't want what it doesn't have.
> Love doesn't strut,
> Doesn't have a swelled head,
> Doesn't force itself on others,
> Isn't always "me first,"
> Doesn't fly off the handle,
> Doesn't keep score of the sins of others,
> Doesn't revel when others grovel,
> Takes pleasure in the flowering of truth,
> Puts up with anything,
> Trusts God always,
> Always looks for the best,
> Never looks back,
> But keeps going to the end (1 Cor. 13:4-8, *The Message*).

The ultimate good work toward which the redemptive grace of God celebrated by Paul in Ephesians 2 is designed to move us; that which is by faith and not of our own doing; the very thing which God prepared beforehand to be our way of life—surely it is to love as we have been loved by God so that others may believe, on the evidence of our transformed behaviors, that he loves them too.

## Notes

1. Marcus Borg, *Meeting Jesus Again for the First Time: The Historical Jesus and the Heart of Contemporary Faith* (San Francisco: Harper, 1995), p.87.

2. Kathleen Norris, *Amazing Grace: A Vocabulary of Faith* (New York: Riverhead Books, 1998), pp.150-151.

3. Neil Alexander, *The Epistles of John* (New York: Macmillan, 1928), pp.32-39.

4. Henri. Nouwen, *Can You Drink the Cup?* (Notre Dame, IN: Ave Maria Press, 1996), pp.72-74.

*Our faith in God who sent his Son to become God-with-us and who, with his Son, sent his Spirit to become God-within-us cannot be real without our faith in the Church. The Church is that unlikely body of people through whom God chooses to reveal God's love for us. Just as it seems unlikely to us that God chose to become human in a young girl living in a small, not very respected town in the Middle East, it seems unlikely that God chose to continue his work of salvation in a community of people constantly torn apart by arguments, prejudices, authority conflicts, and power games. Still, believing in Jesus and believing in the Church are two sides of one faith. It is unlikely but divine!*

—Henri Nouwen

# 5. ENCOURAGEMENT:
## THE ATMOSPHERE FOR GROWTH

*And let us consider how to provoke one another to love and good deeds, not neglecting to meet together, as is the habit of some, but encouraging one another, and all the more as you see the Day approaching*

—Hebrews 10:24-25

Salvation is a personal matter between an individual and the Lord Jesus Christ, but it is most assuredly *not* a private matter. Everyone who is saved through the message of Christ is simultaneously added to the church. So, depending on which metaphor you prefer, anyone who is "born from above" is born into a family—the Family of God; as a member of that family, she is a sister to every other person who has experienced spiritual rebirth. Anyone who is "in Christ" is a member of his body—the Body of Christ; as a part of the body, he has a function to supply for the sake of its total health and productivity. One who has been wooed and won by Christ's love is now included in his bride—the Bride of Christ; as a constituent to that bride, he or she has to take fidelity, partnership, and beauty seriously.

There are countless people who admire the Son of God but

feel that he married beneath himself. So they follow him from a distance. They prefer the safe margins of their house or apartment and watch a religious program on television. They have no qualms about playing golf or fishing every Sunday and will tell you that they think exalted thoughts about Jesus in the serene outdoors. On occasion they may even enjoy light conversation about Christianity with someone who views it the way they do. These same people will tell you in a heartbeat that they want nothing to do with what they call "organized religion" or simply "religion"—as distinguished from spirituality—in their lives. On their view, the Christian religion is cumbersome, flawed, oppressive, embarrassing, and often downright hypocritical. These people value the thought of a "personal relationship with Christ" but want nothing to do with his bride.

The very idea of such a thing is impossible either to find or to defend from Scripture, with its accounts of Christ and his earliest followers. Paul repeatedly insists on the glory of Christ's church as "his body, the fullness of him who fills all in all" (Eph. 1:23). He speaks highly of the church as the "one body" in which "one new humanity" is created—joining Jews, Gentiles, and other alienated groups through his cross (Eph. 2:15-16). It is the true "household of God, built upon the foundation of the apostles and prophets, with Christ Jesus himself as the cornerstone" (Eph. 2:19-20). Indeed, it is a "holy temple in the Lord" and the very "dwelling place for God" on Planet Earth (Eph. 2:21-22). Paul's letter to the Ephesians—as you might have guessed from these phrases taken from its opening sections—presents a high view of the church. It is in this same letter that he later calls the church Christ's bride and declares the bridegroom's intention "to present the church to himself in splendor, without a spot or wrinkle or anything of the kind—yes, so that she may be holy and without blemish" (Eph. 5:22ff).

Paul was no "church-basher"—though he constantly dealt with its problems. He debated its racism and the implications of that ugly spirit for evangelism at a conference in Jerusalem. He battled its earliest doctrinal corruptions at Colossae. He deplored the toleration of immorality in the church at Corinth. On and on the list of church problems known to Paul could go. Yet, with all the other responsibilities he carried as the specially chosen Apostle to the Gentiles, he continually nurtured local churches. "And, besides other things, I am under daily pressure because of my anxiety for all the churches" (2 Cor. 11:28).

So why did Paul continue to affirm the church? Why did he persist in holding forth a positive image of the church? Why did he ask people discouraged with the church's failures to continue to strive for its health and vitality? He understood that the church is central to God's plan for the redemption of humankind. When we get discouraged with the fumbling, stumbling entity we know as church, we must remind ourselves of the same thing. We must raise our line of sight and renew our commitment to making our congregations healthier. We must focus less on one another's flaws and more on the Son of God's perfection. We must envision our local congregations as microcosms of the kingdom of God.

### Learning from Alcoholics Anonymous

The two of us have made the observation more than once that the church could learn a lot from Alcoholics Anonymous. For one thing, there is no top-heavy institutionalism about it. You don't have to get anyone's permission in New York or Washington to form a twelve-step recovery group in your town, neighborhood, or den. You just have to know a few people who want to get sober—or, in its many variations, break free of addiction to drugs, pornography, gambling, etc. Among the many sayings of the group is this one: "All you need to start a new group is two drunks, a coffeepot, and some resentment."

Although there is a headquarters for A.A. in New York, the people there don't like the term "headquarters" and call it instead the General Service Office. "Nobody runs A.A." is the refrain from GSO. "We just provide services to the membership." Almost half the A.A. groups in North America don't even contribute any funds to the New York office for those services. They feel that bearing the expenses of their local groups through voluntary, pass-the-hat donations is enough. Autonomy and decentralization are real concepts with A.A. There is a *laissez-faire* attitude that allows different groups in different countries, sections of a country, or cultural settings within a small region to pursue their own recovery strategies—using the Twelve Steps and Twelve Traditions as guideposts for function rather than edicts for structure. Churches certainly haven't been terribly successful in fostering true autonomy, permitting legitimate cultural adaptation, or using Holy Scripture as revelation rather than law to be decoded authoritatively and enforced rigidly by a defensive hierarchy.

For another, the key to the success of Alcoholics Anonymous is simply honest self-disclosure in a safe setting. You don't have to be sober to join, but you do have to want to be sober. The one thing that can't and won't be tolerated is denial and self-deception about the seriousness of the problem. Neither does anybody get booted out for messing up. If somebody still wants to get better, falling off the wagon is not a barrier to participation—so long as there is continued honesty. "Even if you do slip," an old-timer is likely to say, "there's nobody here who will punish you. The drink is punishment enough."

For our purpose here, however, Alcoholics Anonymous challenges the church to develop an encouraging atmosphere in which people care about one another, rally to support each other, and hold members accountable. Long-time A.A. members sometimes introduce newcomers to a group and say, "You've got to understand that all these folks would be dead if it weren't for each other!" The power of the twelve-step movement is people getting involved with one another. Gordon Grimm, a Lutheran chaplain at a rehab center for alcoholics, had this to say about A.A. in an interview several years ago:

> My personal belief is that we have to get involved with each other. It's what's left out of so much organized religion. For me, a lot of organized religion is escapist—"Just me in the prayer closet." In that caring dimension, the church hasn't done as well as I think A.A. has.
>
> Spirituality has to do with a deep contact with other human beings and with the appreciation that we par-

ticipate in some issues that cannot be rationally explained. For me, spirituality is how I deal with problems, pain, difficulties in my life—I don't have to escape it; there is meaning and purpose in going through rejection and change. Throughout history—all you have to do is read about the religious wars—people have been "doing God's will" by killing somebody else. That's not what spirituality is about. To me, spirituality is living out—the putting into practice—of our greatest responsibility. That responsibility is to love. At their best, the members of A.A. are tying to live up to that responsibility. They are also living out my definition of grace: being loved when we don't deserve it.[1]

Several members of our home church are recovering alcoholics, and a number of twelve-step groups meet in our building each week. When we encounter someone who is battling addiction to alcohol or pornography or gambling—whether that person is a member of our church or not—it is a natural thing to offer to connect him or her with someone who knows that same struggle. With not a single exception, a phone call yields someone who is willing to meet with the new person, get him to the next meeting, introduce him around, and offer him a place in the recovery community.

Once Bill W., Dr. Bob, and a few of the other persons involved in founding Alcoholics Anonymous were explaining it to some advisers to the Rockefeller Foundation. The alcoholics in the room told their stories of recovery. The methods being evolved to reach others were described. One of the men proclaimed, "Why, this is first-century Christianity!" When Bill W. capitalized on that opening and proposed paid missionaries and a chain of hospitals for alcoholics, the same man had the good sense to ask, "But won't money spoil this thing?"[2]

Indeed, there is—in our opinion, at least—a notable similarity between Alcoholics Anonymous and the life of the earliest church. That life centered in house churches where the Lord's Supper was shared around the table, confession of sin took place eye to eye, and people became involved in one another's lives. They attempted, in the words of Paul, to help each other bear their unique burdens. "Bear one another's burdens," he wrote, "and in this way you will fulfill the law of Christ" (Gal. 6:2; cf. Rom. 13:8-10). The half-brother of Jesus reflects this same attitude toward the fundamental link between cultivating a communal atmosphere of looking after one another and Christ's core teachings: "You do well if you really fulfill the royal law according to the scripture, 'You shall love your neighbor as yourself'" (Jas. 2:8; cf. Matt. 22:36-40).

"Brothers, if someone is caught in a sin, you who are spiritual should restore him gently," instructed Paul. "But watch yourself, or you also may be tempted" (Gal. 6:1, NIV). In this verse, the "spiritual" person is not the man or woman who is faultless. Otherwise nobody among us can give assistance to the rest of us. One is "spiritual" in the sense required here only if he or she is a bit more stable on a given day than someone else who is flat on his face. The New Revised Standard Version translates simply "you who have received the Spirit" (Gk, *hoi pneumatikoi*) and leaves open the possibility that anyone who has been saved and in whom the Spirit of God dwells can—without regard to his or her sense of being terribly "spiritual"—show enough Christian love to be concerned, reach out to, and try to reclaim someone who has fallen into a trap Satan has set.

We have thrilled to see A.A. work to restore alcoholics "gently" and have cringed to see churches live up to their reputation of being more judgmental and punitive than helpful. For example, a dentist in the Nashville area who had been in A.A. for three and one-half years—with more than two years of sobriety at the time—decided he needed to come clean with the leaders of his church. After all, he was its music director and the teacher of that church's largest adult Bible class on Sunday. He prayed about it and concluded it was the only honorable and Christ-honoring thing to do.

So the dentist-alcoholic set up a meeting with the church's elders on a Wednesday evening. He told them of his multi-year experience with prescription medications and alcohol, the disaster of a family life he had created for his wife and children, and the decision he had made over three years ago to get help. He told them it had been over two years since he had used a mood-altering chemical stronger than coffee. He gave God the glory for saving his life, reconnecting his family, and giving him the chance to help others—not only through his profession but by encouraging others to get help with their addictions. "Since you are the spiritual shepherds for me and my family," he said, "I believe you have a right to know what I've just told you. I'm asking for you to pray for my continued sobriety. And I hope you will feel free to call on me to help anyone you come across in this church or larger community with a similar problem."

The three men looked at one another. They told the nervous dentist who had just bared his soul to them that they would make arrangements to have someone take his responsibilities for the next Sunday. And they dismissed the meeting without so much as a perfunctory prayer. It is a wonder he didn't leave that meeting and go straight to a liquor store.

None of this is to say that Alcoholics Anonymous is the church, an effective alternative to the church, or always faithful to its own principles. It is simply to say that it models something to the twenty-first century that too many churches seem to have forgotten. Indeed, our sneaking suspicion is that there never would have been an A.A. if the church had been the place of nurture, encouragement, and prayer the church was designed to be.[3]

Indeed, some churches are wonderfully redemptive in their approach to people who are struggling with alcoholism, HIV-infection, divorce, or a thousand other things that disrupt and destroy lives. Across the board, however, Alcoholics Anonymous likely has a better track record—and certainly a better reputation—in the past fifty years than churches. At least, more people go to A.A. and are forthcoming about their desperation than present themselves to churches in full disclosure.

And, yes, there are loving individuals and gracious families in some very cold, austere churches who know how to minister to wounded souls. But such persons should not be outstanding as exceptions within the group. One brother—who has since found another church home—went through the painful failure of his marriage and the public process of having a divorce granted without a single person among his church's nine elders saying so much as a single word to him about his distress. Fortunately, there were several individuals and families outside the church's formal leadership who stayed in close touch with him, who gave him listening ears and sympathetic hearts. Five and a half months after the divorce had been granted, one of the elders finally approached him to ask that he attend a meeting of the full leadership body. Without so much as expressing remorse over what he had been through, it became apparent immediately that the purpose for asking him to meet with them was simply to counsel him against seeking to date any of the women in that church.

Do you think one factor in the church's recent (re)discovery of the power of small groups for Bible study, support, ministry, accountability, and prayer could be what we have witnessed in Alcoholics Anonymous? Do you think a factor in rethinking the duty of spiritual leadership in churches could be that stories such as the ones related above have been all too typical?

Yet the amazing story of Alcoholics Anonymous as a vehicle for support and encouragement falls far short of the divine plan for Christ's church. Twelve-step programs exploit the power of group dynamics for positive ends. They put individuals together in community for the sake of strength—much like the illustration of breaking a single stick but being unable to break a dozen bundled together. But the church has a resource no other group can have so directly and immediately. That resource equips and empowers believers in community for things beyond mere group dynamics. And that resource is, of course, the relational presence of the Holy Spirit—the Spirit present in each believer and binding all to one another and to God.

The personal presence of God indwelling every Christian through the Holy Spirit is a promise of victory to feeble, struggling, overmatched people like us. In spite of anything *behind* you (i.e., in your personal past, in your genetic makeup, in your marital record, in your criminal record, etc.), *around* you (i.e., bad circumstances, poor options, enemies, slander), or *in front of* you (i.e., deadlines, ultimatums, consequences, death), you have something—no, Somebody!—*inside* you who is maximally great, powerful, and loving. You and he joined in the larger community of God's people are a match for anything! God, you, and the relational body to which you have been joined are an overwhelming majority against any and all odds Satan can bring against you. And you have been set into a community of people who are similarly indwelt by the same Spirit.

Collectively, the church is "God's temple" (1 Cor. 3:16) and derives only a secondary energy from the interconnectedness of human spirits and its primary empowerment from the Holy Spirit. So the church—when it functions relationally rather than merely exists as a corporation or independent local franchise—has the ability to equip us for much more than Alcoholics Anonymous has to offer. How have we missed this important promise of Scripture?

We believe in both the need for and power of corporate worship for the people of God (see Chapter 3), but we fear too many Christians have come to expect a "spiritual high" from Sunday mornings that can carry them through the week. That is neither biblical nor practical. The multi-thousand-member church at Jerusalem had not only its occasional big assemblies but its regular house-to-house sharing. There is joy, excitement, and renewed zeal in a large group that helps to confer a sense of identity with others who share the commitment to Jesus Christ; there is study, confession, shared insight, personal challenge, and prayer over special needs in classroom, home, or other small-group settings. We need both to sustain spiritual life over the long haul. We need both as an atmosphere for spiritual growth and maturity. And when the real dynamic for both is the Holy Spirit, the result can only be supernatural.

### Carrying One Another

Getting back to Paul's statement about bearing one another's burdens, there are situations in which one person literally picks up another's load—or even the person himself. Fathers and mothers pick up and carry their babies. Firefighters and paramedics put full-grown adults across their backs or onto stretchers to rescue them from danger. Friends and family do for handicapped persons what four men did for a paralyzed man at Luke 5:17ff. One of the most touching recent accounts of this sort of thing we have seen comes from a 42-year-old tradition at Middlebury College in Vermont.[4]

For more than four decades now, men and women athletes from the school pick up Butch Varno for all the college's basketball and football games. Male and female basketball players get him to the football games. Football players take charge during hoop season. And they literally pick up Butch—all 5' 3" and 170 pounds of him—for the 54-year-old sports fan has cerebral palsy and can do very few things for himself.

> *Above all, maintain constant love for one another, for love covers a multitude of sins.*
>
> —1 Peter 4:8

Butch always wanted to play basketball. He won't, however, because of the devastating disease he has. But during basketball season, student athletes go to his tiny house about a mile off campus, load him into a car, put his wheelchair in the trunk, and get him to the game. Once at the gym, they roll him to his reserved spot at the end of the players bench. Sometimes he gives the pre-game speech: "I love you guys." He holds the game ball during warm-ups and at halftime. Regardless of weather or team record, he seldom ever misses a game.

The players always see to it that Butch gets a hot dog and a Coke. They have to put the hot dog in his mouth, since cerebral palsy has long since taken away the ability to feed himself. "It's kind of weird at first, sticking a hot dog in his mouth," said a 6' 8" forward. "The trick is to throw out the last bite so he doesn't get your fingers." They put the straw in his Coke to his lips. They take him to the bathroom. When Butch gets caught up in the excitement of a game and his arms and upper body begin to thrash the air, they just hold his hands in theirs.

Butch lives with his 73-year-old mother who doesn't drive. And the tradition of student athletes getting involved in Butch Varno's anything-but-easy life traces back to 1961. He was 13 at the time, and his grandmother—a housekeeper at the campus dorms—wheeled Butch to a football game. Sometime around the half, it began to snow. When the game was over, the snow was deep enough that she couldn't push him all the way back to his house. A student named Roger Ralph asked the woman and her ward if they could use a ride. Since that day, Butch has been at the heart of Middlebury athletics.

But it isn't only the athletes who get involved with Butch. Students from the larger student body come by his house practically every day. Over the years, they have taught him to read. They helped him get his GED in 2002—then got him a cap and gown to wear at the party students threw for him to celebrate what he had accomplished. He made a thank-you speech to everybody who was there. Butch wept.

"These kids care what happens to me," says Butch. "I don't know where I'd be without them. Probably in an institution." Indeed, where would *any* of us be without somebody to care about us? And telling a sick or lonely or downright unpleasant and difficult person "God loves you!" rings awfully hollow—until somebody lets God use his hands to help him. Use her lips to talk with her. Use his car or her money or their precious time to make that person feel valuable.

The triune God didn't create people in his image so we could live in dismal isolation from one another. As he has lived from eternity past in the social setting of love among Father, Son, and Holy Spirit, so are human beings created in his likeness meant to live in community. We are supposed to pay attention to one another and to fulfill the royal law by bearing one another's burdens. Sometimes we must bear more than one another's burdens and actually bear one another. And if we must lament that our larger culture is filled with violence, neglect of the poor, and contempt for the weak, God forbid that we live by the same selfish spirit in the Body of Christ!

## Caring for Others: Spiritual Gifts

Have you ever thought of paying attention to others (i.e., support, compassion, a helping hand) as a spiritual gift? In a Pauline list of spiritual skills that includes such notable functions as prophecy, ministry, and teaching is—depending on the translation you read—"showing mercy" (NIV) or being "compassionate" (NRSV). The same list enjoins the spirit of "cheerfulness" as the only appropriate attitude with which caring for others can be exercised as a spiritual, Christ-imitating quality of life (Rom. 12:6-8).

Do you remember the biblical character named Barnabas? He possessed this highly desirable gift. Devoted as he was to loving and honoring God, he dedicated himself to nurturing weak and struggling, cast-off and unwanted souls. This trait of his redeemed personality made him one of the more significant characters in Acts of the Apostles. Interestingly, his original name was simply Joseph, but the apostles gave him the name Barnabas. The name means, according to Luke, "Son of Encouragement" (Acts 4:36). To call someone "son of x" is a well-known Semitic way of identifying the person's most notable quality. That Barnabas lived up to his name is apparent from reading through Acts.

In Acts 4, Barnabas sold a piece of land and donated the proceeds for the apostles to distribute to saints in need. It was unthinkable to him that he should have surplus when others were lacking the basics. In chapter 11, he risked his own reputation to take Saul of Tarsus under his wing and involve him in kingdom activity at Antioch. It was unthinkable to him that someone exhibiting repentance and the desire to join himself to the church should be refused. In chapter 15, he parted company with the now highly respected missionary Paul in order to take a once-failed younger missionary, John Mark, on a preaching tour with him. It was unthinkable to him that the young man's failure should be turned into permanent shame or that he should suffer punishment beyond the anguish of heart he had already endured on account of his lapse of faith. When someone needed a boost of encouragement generated by sincere compassion, he was there.

Ever know anyone like Joseph Barnabas? Over the years, we have been blessed to know several men and women cut from the same bolt of cloth as Barnabas. They encourage young preachers whose sermons are painful to endure. They show up regularly in hospital corridors, nursing homes, and funeral homes. They pay attention to children who don't smile enough or easily. They sacrifice for missionaries, orphans, and people on hard times. They have such compassionate hearts that their eyes tend to moisten easily. When someone needs a listening ear, they make time to listen—no matter how busy they are. And when somebody asks one of these godly people to pray for him or her, you sense immediately that it will be done.

These women have the gift of caring for others. These men are encouragers. They are genuinely compassionate, kindhearted, and benevolent. And they tend to be very quiet and inconspicuous people whose behavior calls attention to others more than to themselves. Theirs is a genuine spiritual gift. The church is God's community in which this gift is imparted, shared, and appreciated. It is the place where healing occurs through self giving love that shows itself as concern (not nosiness), compassion (not pity), and comfort (not enabling indulgence). They are living in authentic spiritual community.

### Prayer as the Instrument of Focus

The means for staying focused on heavenly wisdom, conduct, and community is prayer. Apart from prayer, we are tempted to pursue our ends by our means; bathed in prayer, though, we are inclined to give up plans that do not have Christ as their end and righteousness as their means. The fundamental meaning of "worldliness," in fact, is not partying and debauchery but preoccupation with the things of this passing world of sense experience.

James is helpful here. He teaches about two very different kinds of wisdom—perhaps we would say two very different worldviews—that offer themselves to us every day. One—he calls it "earthly, unspiritual, devilish"—originates with and is championed by the world that is still alienated from God; it promotes success defined in terms of money and power, beauty demonstrated as sex appeal, and self-interest displayed as the willingness to do anything necessary to get what it wants. The other—wisdom "from above"—is God's gift to those who will receive it; it is more interested in purity than pleasure, puts peace above ambition, and is willing to forfeit its rights and turn the other cheek rather than push for having its way.

> Who is wise and understanding among you? Show by your good life that your works are done with gentleness born of wisdom. But if you have bitter envy and selfish ambition in your hearts, do not be boastful and false to the truth. Such wisdom does not come down from above, but is earthly, unspiritual, devilish. For where there is envy and selfish ambition, there will also be disorder and wickedness of every kind. But the wisdom from above is first pure, then peaceable, gentle, willing to yield, full of mercy and good fruits, without a trace of partiality or hypocrisy. And a harvest of righteousness is sown in peace for those who make peace (Jas. 3:13-18).

Remember the definition given earlier of worldliness? It is fundamentally a fixation on things, values, and relationships that are temporal. Worldliness is getting so caught up in things of the five senses that we neglect eternity. The kind of worldliness that typifies too many churches is one that judges their success by numbers, nickels, and nails; a church is successful when it is single-minded about honoring and imitating the Lord Jesus Christ. But what about the larger arena of our lives at school, at work, and in our families? Is it more important to be "cool" or to be holy, to be popular or to be righteous? Is it more important to make money or to do right, to get ahead or to treat people fairly and with respect? Is it more important to make the right friends or to be the right kind of friend, to give your children everything they want or to give them what they really need to be godly people? These choices sound overblown and crazy to many people. Anyone who takes God seriously in this culture knows that they represent very basic choices between competing worldviews.

Christians are subversive to the world's cultural ideals. The prevailing norms in music and entertainment, personal and corporate morality, or family and social ideals run counter to the interests of the kingdom of God. Thus it follows that the only way for Christians to live is in deliberate opposition to the worldview that James labels "earthly, unspiritual, devilish." If that language sounds too harsh to our ears, it is only because we are too influenced by the world. If it is shocking or offensive, it may be that we have compromised our connection with the kingdom of God for the sake of this world. And the single best way to stay oriented to divine realities so as to avoid deception by this-worldliness is prayer. James has already affirmed as much back in the opening lines of his little epistle: "If any of you is lacking in wisdom, ask God, who gives to all generously and ungrudgingly, and it will be given you" (Jas. 1:5). And which type of wisdom do you think God would give in response to prayer?

The fact remains, though, that many of us who claim we want to embrace the worldview of the kingdom of God aren't as prayerful as we should be. And we blame it on God! We say we don't pray because our prayers don't do anything. God doesn't hear us and give us the things we've asked for. "I tried praying about things that mattered to me," somebody says, "and I didn't get what I asked for. So what's the use?"

Perhaps we should be suspicious of this all-too-common

> *Prayer is not wrestling with God's reluctance to bless us; it is laying hold of his willingness to do so.*
>
> —John Blanchard

defense of prayerlessness among Christians. Billy Graham once wrote: "Heaven is full of answers to prayers for which no one ever bothered to ask." Ouch! Could it really be true? When we do pray, are we praying for the wrong things or with a wrong

spirit? Could it be the case that we are even worldly in our
prayers—praying for things that would vindicate us within a system that is fundamentally hostile to God rather than praying
within the divine worldview for things he would never refuse to
grant? God will always give one of his children what he or she
requests within his will—or something far better than we even
thought to request.

You may have as much of God's heart, favor, and blessing
as you are willing to receive in this life. Christ has opened the
way to his treasure-chamber by his own blood, and he invites us
to take all we want. When we pray in his name, we are assured
that we will be heard—and answered. Yet our spiritual poverty
is often comparable to that of a man who has been invited into
the vaults of Fort Knox and given permission to carry out as
much bullion from the gold reserves of the United States as he
needs. He would not be a thief to fill his hands, his pockets, a
bag. He has been invited inside and given *carte blanche* to
everything in the vault. So whose fault will it be if he walks out
empty-handed or having picked up only a gum wrapper and
cigarette butt he saw lying on the vault floor?

In the same way, it is nobody's fault but ours if we live in
spiritual poverty. If we choose to use—or, more correctly,
waste—our prayers asking for a successful career, huge amounts
of money, fabulous notoriety, and good health, aren't we asking
for gum wrappers and cigarette butts when we could be asking
for and getting valuable things? Even to say such a thing sounds
shocking, for we think so much like the world. Those *are* the
valuable things. Are they not? What does Scripture say? Can you
think of a single line in the Word of God that would support
such a claim?

### The Trauma of Unanswered Prayers

When someone thinks he is being neglected or overlooked,
worldly wisdom tells him to invest his prayers in asking for a
promotion, a raise, or a wife who will appreciate him. When
someone fears that age or diminished beauty will let life pass her
by, worldly wisdom tells her to act like a girl again and to prove

she can still turn heads. When someone has been living above his means and saddled himself with unmanageable debts, worldly wisdom instructs him to pray for a lightning strike at the casino or to land a big account for the sake of the bonus it would bring. When someone is seriously ill, worldly wisdom tells her to pray to be healed and spared from suffering and death. But what did James say about the wisdom of this world?

Wisdom from above, on the other hand, might lead the overlooked soul to pray for an unselfish spirit and to be satisfied with the certainty of God's love in Christ. Wisdom from above would move the aging beauty queen to care less about her figure and to pray for the "lasting beauty of a gentle and quiet spirit, which is very precious in God's sight"(1 Pet. 3:4). Wisdom from above might cause the saddled-with-debt soul to simplify life, refocus priorities, and pray henceforth to be kept "free from the love of money" and to learn to "be content with what you have" (Heb. 13:5a). Wisdom from above will cause the sick woman to pray for faith, courage, and dignity in the midst of her ordeal.

Don't misunderstand. Don't miss the point. Of course we may pray for the distressing aspects of this temporal life, but we must neither center nor exhaust our visits to heaven's treasure vault on such things. Otherwise, like the Prodigal Son, we have taken our access to the Father's wealth and squandered its power. It is only people "who are depraved in mind and bereft of the truth," maintains Spirit-guided Paul, "who think that godliness is a means of gain" (1 Tim. 6:5)—or perpetual health, youth, or press coverage.

At the end of his epistle, James will say that the prayer of a righteous person is "powerful and effective" both for the seeking of forgiveness at God's throne and for weather conditions (Jas. 5:16-17). But which is more important: pardon for sin or compliant weather? And what made Elijah's prayers about withholding and sending rain effective: righteous submission in seeking God's will or selfish concern to have a bumper crop and pay off his note at the bank?

Could it be that the primary hindrance to prayer is the confusion of worldviews? Prayer is not a means for manipulating

God to our ends. Prayer is not a free pass that exempts Christians from problems. Prayer is not the means to the end of selfish ambition—even if that selfish ambition is masked under appropriate religious language. Yes, we pray from the world of temporal experience and limited understanding. But we are praying to the Holy God of Heaven and Earth whose promise to hear our prayers takes into account more things than we will ever know. And we must trust him to do what he has promised—to hear, to answer, to do more than we could ever know to request. So not *our* will, Father, but *yours* be done! Jesus is our perfect example again on this point. As someone put it: "When Jesus prayed to the one who could save him from death, he did not get that salvation; he got instead the salvation of the world!"

> *Prayer at its highest is a two-way conversation—-and for me the most important part is listening to God's replies.*
>
> —Frank C. Laubach

Pray. And try to pray by the guidance of wisdom from above rather than earthly, unspiritual or even devilish wisdom. God of love that he is, he would not have commanded us to pray if there is no purpose to it. And pray with the assurance that God's failure to respond to your prayers is only apparent rather than real, for—even when you do not have the answers you requested or had hoped to see—you still have *him*. And he is always enough. More than enough.

So perhaps the wisdom of certain Christian mystics comes into view here. They write and speak of "listening prayer"—an oxymoron among most Christians. But is that not what the Psalmist suggests with these words: "Be still and know that I am God"? (Psa. 46:10). There is an element to all conversation that requires not just speaking but active listening. By that we are suggesting more than the aggressive incorporation of reading Scripture in our devotional life. We are suggesting that there is great blessing in being still before the Lord, opening our hearts and minds to the experience of presence precisely because we do not have the necessary words. We trust in the promise of the Spirit's groanings on our behalf (Rom. 8:26-27).

Listening prayer also means that we listen with discerning hearts for God's answers to our requests. Sometimes the clear answer of God to an earnest prayer "according to his will" (cf. 1 John 5:14-15) is to deny a job or promotion or ministry. To allow no healing to take place and to allow cancer to have its natural outcome. To bring no last-minute rescue to a disintegrating marriage. Listening prayer is the sort that can receive these answers: Honor God from a place of humility, denial, and need. Give him glory by bearing your pain with dignity, grace, and faith. Receive his loving answer through the ministry of others. Be faithful unto death. Endure loss as spiritual discipline. In losing the faithful love of one you trusted, rest more securely in the love that cannot fail.

Listening prayer is frightening. It is non-manipulative and altogether risky. It not only concedes to but rejoices in the sovereignty of God—and waits. And struggles. And trusts. And knows he is always enough. More than enough.

### Wonderful Things Happen Here

For the moment, then, let's assume that we grasp the following:

- Lone Ranger Christianity is an oxymoron, for God has set every man and woman he has saved by Christ's blood into that living entity known as the Bride of Christ, his church.

- In spite of all her flaws, Christ loves his bride wholeheartedly and redemptively.

- Churches today that want to be less institutional and more relational can learn a great deal from watching Alcoholics Anonymous to see how supportive and healing community is created.

- Christian community involves bearing one another's burdens and creating a safe atmosphere for spiritual growth.

- Barnabas-type encouragement through compassion, risk-taking for the sake of others, and giving second chances to people who fail is a superior and more Christ-like strategy for a church than the judgment, defensiveness, and exclusion for which churches have been known.

- Communities of encouragement, healing, and hope can be founded only among people with a worldview that is radically different from the one that dominates our culture.

- Prayer is the means by which God refines our perspective on reality, imparts a new worldview, and teaches us to trust him.

- Prayer is also the primary means by which we encourage one another as we learn together to embrace a kingdom lifestyle, affirm it to one another, and wait for the unfolding of the drama that will end with Christ's glorious return.

*If* we really grasp these things, wonderful things will happen in our churches. We will be anything but cold, austere groups of dour-faced religionists. We will be people who know we are together by God's purpose. No, we are not an ideal community, but—as with Noah's family on a creaky, stinky boat—this is the only safe place for us. But we want to be increasingly attractive to the unbelieving world around us by exhibiting the settled joy and radiant beauty of a bride to her beloved! So we model acceptance, responsibility, and progress over time. And we pray for God to be graciously present in our midst to work this trans-forming miracle in another generation of his people.

*First, we will look for ways to encourage, support, cheer, and contribute to one another's spiritual growth and progress.* The world naturally lapses into competition out of the selfishness of the fallen nature. A distinctive feature of a life under the reign of God is its unselfish desire to see others advance. Leaders want to develop new, younger leaders who are better equipped than they were to model and teach the gospel of grace. Older saints want to see younger ones mature, take responsibility, and do well. Sinners in recovery tell their stories both to warn the young, invite the hesitant, and encourage the faint-hearted.

*Second, we will celebrate success in our midst.* Beyond praying for others with an unselfish heart, it is important to give honor where honor is due. This means not only taking note of special events in family life (e.g., births, graduations, significant career achievements, etc.) but paying special attention to spiritual struggle that issues in victory. One of the most obvious values of testimonies shared in church assemblies is to allow the entire body to rejoice with those who are rejoicing. It is more spiritually valuable to celebrate a marital reconciliation, the anniversary of someone's sobriety, or the presence of someone for whom the church has been in prayer (e.g., missionary, one who has been critically ill, etc.) than paying off a mortgage or buying a new bus.

*Third, we will be eager to comfort, reassure, and stir hope in one another.* In addition to growth, progress, and success, every church also has its experiences of tragedy. There is the death of some key person whose experience and wisdom have been invaluable over the years; there is the death of an infant whose loss staggers a young mother and father who had prayed so long to have a child. There is a painful divorce. Someone is diagnosed with advanced cancer. A person is arrested and exposed in the press as a corporate thief. It is one thing to celebrate success and take pride in the people of your church. Can you stand with those who need friends in their crisis times and failures? These are the people who need to hear the gospel message of hope afresh.

*Fourth, we will learn to practice hospitality with one another.* If hospitality to strangers is a virtue (cf. Heb. 13:2), isn't it reasonable to suppose we are to show the same spirit toward those we know best? And isn't it also reasonable to suspect that some of the primary events of encouragement and prayer that sustain Christians will occur in these situations where we share our homes, tables, and life stories with one another? We recommend that houses, apartments, and dorm rooms be transformed into centers of warmth, confidentiality, and prayer among believers. Host small groups for Bible studies. Offer your living space for committee meetings or work groups. Integrate your personal life and that of your family with people whose life values and Christian commitments are compatible with your own. It is a form of validation, reinforcement, and encouragement to faith.

*Fifth, we will hold one another accountable in love.* The hardest thing for us to do is the hardest thing for you to do: confront. Both families and churches are dysfunctional when they cannot name and deal with their problems. And if the problem is pride or jealousy or impurity, you can count on it coming wrapped in a person! Pretend it isn't happening, and it only gets worse; the person dies spiritually—and probably infects several others with the same spiritual disease. We must love one another enough to hold each other accountable before God. It is *not* a loving thing to look the other way when somebody is bent on spiritual self-destruction. It *is* a loving thing to go to someone who has been seduced into one of Satan's traps and try to restore that brother or sister. Go prayerfully. Go confessionally. Go sorrowfully. But go.

*Sixth, we will confer and seek forgiveness easily, gracefully, and openly.* A high percentage of those who are confronted over sin—especially when the accountability factor is introduced earlier rather than later—will respond positively. They don't like what they are doing. And they certainly don't like the alienation and pain that sin is beginning to introduce into their lives. Confronted with the fact that their behavior isn't hidden from view and convinced that the person(s) doing the intervention really love them, believe better of them, and want to support them in recovery, they tend to confess not only their illicit behavior but their desire to be forgiven and healed. God communicates his grace to such people through a church community that has established a pattern of asking and giving pardon. As people of love, we keep no record of wrongs. We do not humiliate or punish wrongdoers. In the spirit of James 5:16, we have learned that being confessional about failure puts it into the light of God's grace for healing. The church not only prays for healing but fosters it by ongoing attention to one another in love.

*Seventh, we will help one another die well.* The final act of the Christian drama to be played out in the church on Planet Earth is death. It is understandable that unbelievers find it hard to talk about dying, be with one another through the process of dying, and feel nothing but profound sadness in its wake. Christians subscribe to a worldview that means death is hardly the worst thing that could happen to someone! If we really believe what Scripture says about death, we will not grieve as those who have no hope beyond this life. We will, instead, affirm that the resurrection of the Son of God in the power of the Holy Spirit has guaranteed our own triumph over the grave. Part of the striking beauty of the church in our time would be for us not only to call funerals "celebrations of life" but to deal with terminal illness, the process of dying, and the death event in distinctively Christian ways so as to help each other die well. And dying well means honesty about terminal illness, candor about our anxieties over pain and suffering, affirmation of Christ's personal conquest of death, lament in the face of loss, and confidence in our hope of the life that is to come. This is obviously a communal process for people of faith.

> *Optimism means faith in men, in their human potential; hope means faith in God and in his omnipotence.*
>
> —Carlo Carretto

## Conclusion

Newspapers across America and the major television networks made a celebrity out of a young man in the fall of 2002 who still doesn't understand what all the fuss is about. His name is Jake Porter, and he was only 17 at the time. What happened around him on that October night in a football stadium is an illustration of how churches should operate as environments for spiritual growth.[5]

Jake and his family moved from Dayton to McDermott, Ohio, when he was 13 years old. The move put him in a school district that allows children with special needs to be part of the customary life of kids their age. So Jake, who has a disorder known as "Chromosomal Fragile-X"—the most common cause of inherited mental retardation—went to school with people his own age who had learned how to treat him appropriately. And he thrived. By the time he started high school, he was already one of the most popular kids in his class.

Coach Dave Frantz admitted him to Northwest High School's football squad when he started ninth grade. In spite of the fact that Jake never took a snap in a real game over the four years that followed, the happy boy with a bubbly personality, huge amounts of energy, and a short attention span showed up for practice every day. He dressed in full uniform for every game. He even had his own special play, "84-iso," that the team would run occasionally in practices. With his high school career about to end, Coach Frantz wanted Jake finally to get to play. It was going to happen on October 18, 2002.

Northwest was playing Waverly that night, and Frantz had talked to his coaching counterpart earlier. He explained that Jake couldn't be hit. "If the game's not at stake on the last play," he had said, "I wanted him to come in and take a knee." Waverly was leading 42-0 with only five seconds left in the game. In a timeout before they were to run out the clock, coach Derek DeWitt of Waverly offered to go the plan one better and let Jake score a touchdown. The agreement was struck. The officials were notified of what was about to happen.

Coach Frantz sent Jake into the game at tailback. At Waverly's 49-yard line, "84-iso" was called in the huddle. When the ball was snapped and handed off to Jake Porter, the remaining twenty-one players on the field all stepped back and opened a huge hole in front of him. He went through, turned back toward the original line of scrimmage, and unquestionably was confused. "84-iso" had always been practiced as a play in which Jake would simply down the ball.

His teammates from Northwest pointed down the field toward Waverly's end zone. Then the Waverly defenders—who were passing on the chance to shut out an opponent—began cheering him too! *Both* teams wound up escorting Jake on his 49-yard run to daylight—cheered as well by players on the sidelines and by fans from both schools in the bleachers. It took him about ten seconds to get there. And there wasn't a dry eye in the stadium.

Unselfishness is always a highlight event in sports—and in life generally—because it is so unusual. It must be the rule rather than the exception in the life of the Bride of Christ. It is part of her beauty before a watching world to see the appealing alternative of a spiritual culture that not only tolerates but makes achievers out of people with such limited abilities. It is the way of the community of faith. The community of grace. The community of encouragement that sustains its life through prayer.

### Notes

1. Quoted in Nan Robertson, *Getting Better. Inside Alcoholics Anonymous* (New York: William Morrow, 1988), pp. 143-144.

2. Robertson, *Getting Better,* p. 68.

3. Most people are aware that Alcoholics Anonymous is indebted to a Christian movement initially known as the First Century Christian Fellowship and later the Oxford Group. Bill W. attended its meetings and built on its precepts of surrender, confession, restitution, prayer, and assistance to others in verbalizing what would later be known as the Twelve Steps. Early on, in fact, "Alcoholics Anonymous was a more conventionally religious society. Among other things, its pioneers prayed together on their knees." [Robertson, *Getting Better,* p. 141.] One of the reasons this practice was abandoned was that it was a barrier to involvement with A.A. for those who were non-religious in background and, more tellingly, to many who had been judged, rejected, or otherwise hurt by traditional religions.

4. Rick Reilly, "Extra Credit," *Sports Illustrated*, March 10, 2003, p. 82.

5. Information taken from James Walker, "Act of kindness speaks volumes about football's spirit," *The (Huntington, WV) Herald-Dispatch*, October 24, 2002; James Walker, "Porter's inspirational story draws national attention," *Herald-Dispatch*, November 7, 2002; and James Walker, "Human touch," *Herald-Dispatch*, November 10, 2002.

*Religions are man's search for God; the gospel is God's search for man. There are many religions, but one gospel.*

—E. Stanley Jones

*As we go to the cradle only in order to find the baby, so we go to the scriptures only to find Christ.*

—Martin Luther

# 6. GOSPEL:
## THE LEGITIMATING MESSAGE

*For I am not ashamed of the gospel; it is the power of God for salvation to everyone who has faith, to the Jew first and also to the Greek. For in it the righteousness of God is revealed through faith for faith; as it is written, "The one who is righteous will live by faith."*
—Romans 1:16-17

Paul's theme sentence to the Romans should serve as a constant reminder to all who seek to proclaim the good news of Jesus Christ that the power of salvation always has been, is, and always will be about the righteousness of God revealed by God and enabled by God. Even faith itself in Romans 1:16-17 seems to have more to do with God's activity than our own human understandings. All who claim a place in the heritage of Christian faith can agree on the gospel's capacity to evoke change in peoples' lives. But agreement on the power of the gospel—and even the necessity of faith—often leaves many assumptions within our faith unquestioned and unintelligible.

Think about the mental image that most often comes to mind when we use the word God. We sing about a God who is alive, a God who has acted in loving, redeeming ways. The Bible is full of different names for God that reflect various attributes of his nature. We use large words to characterize the infinite mystery we are trying to seize with our minds. We talk about the "omni-God" who is all-knowing and all-powerful and everywhere-present. We speak of his transcendence and immanence. But most of us live with particular metaphors that are the controlling images for our reflections on God. We struggle with living in paradox and mystery because we seek clarity in our understanding. So which is he: Distant and wholly other? Or closer to us than the blood in our veins? Perhaps your primary image is of the Loving Father or Caring Shepherd. Perhaps it is the notion of the Awesome Creator. Perhaps your primary impression of God is that of a dispassionate or angry judge looking for a reason to find you guilty and condemn you. Even if that is not primary, it may be a lingering memory that still haunts you from time to time.

Think next about your image of the Christ. We speak and sing of him as Son of God. We know him as Savior and Friend, Redeemer and Lord. We speak of his divine identity and his human identity. We struggle to comprehend both of those identities being simultaneous. We need to make sense of Paul's words in Colossians 1:15-20 and his words in Romans 1:1-7. Was he declared Son of God through his resurrection from the dead (Rom. 1: 4)? Was he the firstborn of all creation through whom all things were created (Col. 1:15)? That is, in using the language of Paul, shall we focus on the human Jesus declared Son of God by his resurrection? Or shall we focus on the divine Christ who is from the beginning? The contrast in these two verses points to a larger struggle to speak openly and honestly about the divine and human co-existing at once in the person of Jesus.

Too often in our struggle to understand Jesus' dual nature we think of his humanity when we need to be thinking of his divinity, and vice versa.[1] Think about the most dominant of those words or images in your mind at this very moment. If you were to describe exactly what Jesus did for you as Savior, what would you say? Would you talk about the debt of sin you owed and the way in which your sins are forgiven because Jesus died in your place? Would you talk about the fact that in his death and resurrection Jesus conquered death itself? Would you talk about his life as model for how you yourself are trying to live? Maybe all of the above? But is there one image that dominates the others?

Now consider your image of church. We don't sing about the church all that much, but we do talk about church—often borrowing the language and images articulated by Paul when we wish to speak in ideal terms. But the reality of our experiences more often gives us quite different images and conversations. We know the negative, cynical perceptions of church that we sometimes encounter from those who have no connections with it. Do our images spring from contemporary consumer models where we fit our offerings to a "target audience"? Do we unconsciously have business models by which we operate and explain our existence? Is the church therefore like a machine—to be explained and operated mechanically?

What is your primary impression of the church? Is it Paul's vision for the "body of Christ" or "bride of Christ"? Is church primarily a means of identifying the other "insiders"—the people who think about religious topics the same way you do? There are other churches where people think differently than us, and that's all right—or perhaps not. Is church, in one sense at least, like a club membership with special entrance requirements? Is it an organization with a particular belief system to which individuals subscribe in order to join and belong? Does being part of such a group suggest inclusion

> *For I handed on to you as of first importance what I in turn had received: that Christ died for our sins in accordance with the scriptures, that he was buried, and that he was raised on the third day in accordance with the scriptures.*
>
> —1 Corinthians 15:3-4

as well as exclusion? When you hear the phrase "member of the church," what do you think?

Consider your thought processes and vocabulary with regard to salvation. Who are the leading characters in the drama of our salvation? We might quickly say, "God and his Son, of course!" So what is the role of our own decision-making? When we adopt Paul's line again, "You were saved by grace through faith," what does salvation accomplish? Is it only about forgiveness of sins? Does it entail life after death? Is it relevant to the transformation of our present human circumstances? Is the free gift of God that we label grace simply an all-encompassing fire insurance policy?

Finally, think about your perception of Holy Scripture. We may all agree that it is "God's Word"—but what do we mean by that? What is our primary image of the Bible? Is it an ancient artifact that church people keep dressing up in new translations and study editions for shelf decorations? Is it God's instruction manual for human behavior, or better yet, God's rulebook for life? Perhaps, like our predecessors of 200 years ago, we think of it more as the foundational document for life—a constitution, if you will, comparable to our nation's foundational document. What is the dominant image that comes to mind?

What gives the Bible authority? When we use words like infallible or inerrant, what are we seeking to accomplish or preserve? When we say that the Bible is true, what kind of truth claims are we making? Is this philosophical truth? Scientific truth? Literal, historical truth—a veritable videotape history? When we use Paul's words from 2 Timothy 3:16, that "all Scripture"— which in this case could only have referred to something akin to our Old Testament—is "God-breathed," what does that mean? How are the various translations to be understood in relation to this idea? If we are the target audience for the Scripture, what are we expected to take from it? Is it God's instruction manual for human behavior? Do we think of Scripture as the story of God and his interaction with his creation? But what difference does that make? And is the Bible difficult or easy to understand? Do we have parts we like and parts we ignore?

## Exploring Our Assumptions

To think deeply and seriously about the sources of our images for God and Christ—or the Holy Spirit, who is to most of us even more mysterious and distant—quickly leads to some assumptions that we seldom explore. Yet it is our images and understandings of God and Christ and church and Scripture that ultimately set in motion our message. We use the word *gospel* all the time in church circles. It's the Good News! Good news about what? Well, about salvation, of course! Salvation from what? What are we trying to be saved from or for? What are we trying to save others from? Why should anyone desire this salvation we are offering?

Are we trying to save people for a life after death that they don't believe in anymore because that's just all ancient superstition anyway? Are we trying to save people from their sins, a word which holds little meaning or threat to our existence anymore because we have redefined sin as disease or psychological or behavioral disorder or simply dismissed the concept as a religious effort to strip the fun out of life? What is it that salvation "does" for a person? And when people look around at churches here in our towns and cities on Sundays—or Tuesdays for that matter—what does being saved contribute to their existence? What is the "good news"?

We asked you to think about your images of God, Christ, and Scripture because most of us have collections of images, and we know subconsciously that none of them is adequate. When we try to think or speak of an infinitely "other" being who created and sustains our world, we only have inadequate words and images. But at different times, different images dominate. We often end up with strange mixtures of images, and it quickly gives one a headache to try to sort them out. For example, while a person would not view God as judge most of the time, that same person may have a dominant view of the death of Jesus that is focused on God the Judge needing justice to be served regarding human sin. "Jesus died for my sins; he took my sins and paid the price for them at the cross." You know the song: "He paid a debt he did not owe; I owed a debt I could not pay…" In saying or singing such sentiments, we conceive of God as judge and the death of Jesus as the just punishment required by the judge for our lawlessness. Only occasionally do we stop and ask why God needed to be so exacting with that justice when we want his grace to be so all-encompassing after the fact. And in such a scenario, grace seems to function principally as superior fire insurance—protecting us from hell when we otherwise deserve its punishment. Grace becomes the "King's X" that amounts to a get-out-of-jail-free card.

Then there is all our confusion about church and kingdom. The church is the manifestation of God's reign on the earth, but surely that's not all there is to the kingdom. The once-simple equation of church and kingdom is constantly frustrated by our less than kingdom-like behavior, both corporately and individually. There is renewed interest in our time in talking about the reign of God, the kingdom of God, as a call to discipleship, spiritual disciplines, and accountability. But much of that very quickly starts sounding and feeling like someone reacting to cheap grace with a new set of rules.

> *The Bible is alive, it speaks to me; it has feet, it runs after me; it has hands, it lays hold on me.*
>
> —Martin Luther

Can you hear the dilemma? At some level, one can find all of these components in Scripture. But there is much more to God and Jesus and salvation in the Bible than this set of legal images. There is more to the activity of Jesus on the cross than the image of penal substitution. There are other images that have been dominant in church history besides the idea that the enemy is sin and God the Judge has to have justice served for our transgressions of divine law. That is only one window for understanding a much more complex event.

So where do we begin to sort this out, so that Good News can really be good news to the world of our time? Without belittling any persons or events in our past, we believe that—before we can adequately announce the Good News in our time—we need to address the conflicts that have arisen in our thinking about Scripture, God, and human salvation through a couple of centuries of development in which these mixed metaphors have come to us through the osmosis of church and culture in America. To use yet another metaphor, we have reached a point in the life of a house in which two sets of shingles have already served their purpose and it is time for a new set to be put on. However, that third set cannot simply be layered on the first two. The roofing contractor first has to strip the first two layers off in order to put down the new one. It is the same with our world, our faith, and the assumptions we carry about so uncritically; it is time to take off some layers in order to begin building afresh.

## Stripping Back the Layers

We believe the place to start thinking afresh about the Good News is in the way in which we understand Scripture itself. Our modern day translations and the common-sense reasoning approach to reading both have their beginnings in the fifteenth and sixteenth centuries with the Reformation and the dawn of what has come to be called the Enlightenment.

It is important to recognize that the "new world" being created in the church through people like Martin Luther (1483-1546), John Calvin (1509-1564), and Ulrich Zwingli (1484-1531) coincided with a much larger "new world" being announced by the mathematical calculations and astronomic discoveries of Copernicus (1473-1543) and Galileo (1564-1642). It was not simply that the Christian church was undergoing a reformation through these protesters; the human understanding of the universe was undergoing a revolution. Just as the Roman Catholic Church had been in place for more than a thousand years, so there had been a "scientific" understanding of the heavens and earth that had been taken for granted as the biblical worldview for over a thousand years. It was the universe as first conceived by the astronomer Ptolemy in the second century A.D. In his configuration, Planet Earth was at the center of ten crystalline spheres; the sun, moon, and planets represented the inner spheres, with the remotest sphere reserved for stars and space—and God. For a thousand years, the Roman Church accepted this understanding of the world and read the Bible through that lens—and vice versa.

It is little wonder that Copernicus and Galileo were considered heretics by the church. It wasn't just the overthrow of geocentrism (i.e., Earth as center of the universe) that was at stake. God and the Bible were lost if Copernicus and Galileo were correct because people so completely connected the Ptolemaic universe to the Bible. However, there was a dominant metaphor for God that was part of the "spirit of the age" in the sixteenth century that served as the means for overcoming the fear of the new world order. That was the image of God as Judge and Lawgiver. One can see this dominant image in the artistry of Michelangelo's "Last Judgment" (1535-41). It is certainly obvious in Martin Luther's reading of Romans and Galatians that led him to "justification (i.e., a legal term) by faith." It can even be seen in an edition of a Catholic Bible in 1486—the printing press came along in 1454—in which the cover page "The New Testament" was first added to distinguish between legal covenants in Holy Scripture.

Later, in the sixteenth and seventeenth centuries, philosophers such as Francis Bacon (1561-1626) and Rene Descartes (1596-1650) developed a focus on human reason as the center for perceiving and knowing all truth.[2] Sir Isaac Newton (1643-1727) made official the discoveries of his predecessors when he explained the "laws of nature" (1687). His use of the word "law" is at the heart of seeing God as the Great Lawgiver. One can only wonder what might have been had he chosen instead to speak, as Brian McLaren suggests, of the "grammar of nature" or the "harmonics of nature." Important to our discussion here is the momentous choice of the word "law." The connotations attached to the notion of "God the Lawgiver" allowed the Christian world to adopt the new universe of Galileo a couple of centuries after the church had condemned both him and Copernicus to death for their heresy. But this "rescue" would eventually exact a high toll in recasting many features of Christian discourse.

By the seventeenth and eighteenth centuries, the new world of America was being populated by people in search of religious and political freedom. The emphasis on human reason as the power to discern all truth meant that every individual had certain "unalienable rights" in this country. Both governments and churches would not be structured according to the traditions and patterns of the world from which people had fled in search of freedom.

The same ideals that framed our nation's democratic government were framing both personal religious convictions and churches.[3] A premium was placed on every individual's right to read the Bible for oneself, to decide for oneself. This meant that every person had the same access to understanding, and the same "right to be right" as any other person—regardless of life-circumstances. The newborn Christian was as capable of preaching the gospel as the person whose life had been spent in study. Both opinions, if reasoned well, were of equal weight.

The Bible was indeed the most popular reading in our nation at the time, as evidenced by literally hundreds of editions of Scripture being produced. There were certain ways of reading the Bible that were held in common by the vast majority of Christian people in America by the beginning of the nineteenth century. Mark Noll[4] suggests that there were three dominant rules of interpretation at work among those who came from a Reformed tradition: (1) the belief that the Bible alone was to be followed over against other religious authorities; (2) most Christians practiced some version of the "Regulative Principle," an idea developed through the Puritans which held that "believers were required to do what the Bible commands but were equally required to not do those things about which the Bible is silent"; and (3) the Bible's teachings on morality provided a blueprint for how Christians should live in response to God's salvation.

While these rules for biblical interpretation were not accepted by Anglican and Lutheran believers, one can sense their shaping presence on the thought world of Scripture for those who became leaders in the Restoration Movement.[5] The problem with this approach to reading the Word of God—an individualist reading shaped by fixed rules of interpretation—came when there was no consensus opinion reached about the meaning of a particular text or issue. The only recourse left when reasoning together produced different answers was to assume that the other party was simply wrong—by virtue of either ignorance or dishonesty. In either case, a harsh judgment was passed against a brother or sister. Fellowship was put into jeopardy. Other negative judgments came more easily. Thus, even those groups whose ultimate interest might be unity were constantly facing the prospect of a disagreement that would reach divisive proportions. For the nation as a whole and for the majority of churches, that issue was slavery.

## Our Restoration Heritage

It is vitally important that we understand the place of great thinkers like Thomas and Alexander Campbell and Barton W. Stone in this larger world of ideas and religious practice in the early days of democracy in America. At a time in our nation's history when the Constitution (1787) and Bill of Rights (1891) were shaping forces in our thinking about government of, by, and for the people, it should not surprise us that Thomas Campbell wrote in the *Declaration and Address* (1809) that "The Church of Christ upon earth is essentially, intentionally, and constitutionally one." A bit later in the same document, he stated more precisely what is meant by constitutional: "the New Testament is as perfect a constitution for the worship, discipline and government of the New Testament Church, and as perfect a rule for the particular duties of its members, as the Old Testament was for the worship, discipline, and government of the Old Testament Church, and the particular duties of its members."

One can immediately hear not only the parallel use of the word "constitution" with our national interests but also a not-so-subtle distinction being made in the value of the two parts of Scripture—Old and New Testaments.[6] This constitutional approach to reading the New Testament was significant. It fit well with our nation's claims to identity and unity as a nation with the Constitution as the foundational document. The New

Testament was to serve the church in the same way. The troubling aspect of the comparison comes, however, in the realization that the primary lens through which one reads our nation's Constitution is judicial. The interpreters of the Constitution are immediately cast as lawyers and judges. It is the foundation of our legal system.

Such a reading of the New Testament necessarily invited a reading that sorted through the narrative events in search of the propositional rules for "worship, discipline, and government" of the church. The search for rules later underwent a further reductionism when people began to debate just when the "new" testament/covenant really began.[7] The day of Pentecost in Acts 2 became the line of demarcation for some, thus relegating the Gospels to the same background status as the Old Testament. Never mind the fact that the Gospels were all written by Christians for Christian audiences in the middle to late first century.

When Thomas' son, Alexander, later offered a more systematic understanding of the Christian faith, he summarized his section on rules for biblical interpretation with these words: "The Bible is a book of facts, not of opinions, theories, abstract generalities, nor of verbal definitions. It is a book of awful facts, grand and sublime beyond description."[8] Such language reflects Campbell's debt to John Locke, whom he admired greatly. Sometimes referencing him by the title "The Philosopher," Campbell took his epistemology almost entirely from the great empiricist thinker. Just as Locke rejected Cartesian Rationalism, so Campbell was inevitably forced to call into question its theological counterpart in Calvinism. Thus a "fact" was neither intuitive nor obtainable by a direct operation of the Holy Spirit. The mind's *tabula rasa* (i.e., blank tablet) received facts through the mediation of Spirit-given revelation in the Bible; it was the duty of reason alone—maintaining strict objectivity, refusing to be influenced by tradition, and rejecting bias—to take simple facts in order to discern complex truths. The complex truths derived at the end of these often-arduous paths of reasoning by syllogism were accounted as rock-solid as the simple facts with which one began.[9]

Campbell and his heirs, while calling for objectivity and freedom from bias, were nonetheless children of their own time and place. They were Enlightenment thinkers. They elevated reason above all as the final arbiter of truth. So it should come as no surprise that the search for "facts" was conducted as one would any other literature claiming to have authority for human behavior. One searched for those actions expressly commanded in the document. Or, lacking a black-letter command, one searched for obvious examples of approved actions in the New Testament that were to be enjoined on Christians—for there was a presumption of an underlying command to those examples.

> *If the gospel does not consist of bare facts and commands, neither is the church an inanimate object. It is the body of Christ, a living, breathing organism, and living bodies can survive many wounds and live with many imperfections. Live bodies can contract diseases and recover, even lose body parts and remain vibrantly alive.*
>
> —Leonard Allen

Issues of inference and silence in the New Testament—at least for Thomas Campbell—were always to be considered matters of opinion that should not be bound on others. However, some of the heirs to the Campbells' approach to Scripture were not so gracious about inference. In good Aristotelian-Lockean tradition, they held that reasoning correctly about the simple facts was certain to produce conclusions as sound as their premise-facts. Thus they came to speak of "*necessary* inferences" and gave them the same status as tests of fellowship as the New Testament's explicit commands and approved examples.

Again, not wanting to impugn the motives of any of these great thinkers—or any of the people who followed over the next two centuries—this view of Scripture led to an increasingly legal-judicial reading (i.e., commands, examples, inferences) of a shrinking collection of texts (i.e., Acts and the Epistles) within the larger whole.[10] It has the effect of reducing Scripture from a grand narrative that portrays the story of God's redemptive love to our human search for rules about right behavior with regard to salvation, worship, church organization, and discipline. Keeping the rules in these areas validated faithfulness and differentiated identity from others who did not live under the same collection of rules. The rule of silence and the blueprint understanding of Scripture took on greater force among many who sought with special urgency to clarify the rules for worship. People in Churches of Christ were by no means the only group reading Scripture through this lens. Many others also came to understand all or part of the Bible as *God's Instruction Manual*.[11]

Scripture is so much more than that! Once we back away from that human-centered search for the rules by which we may judge ourselves and others, we discover afresh that the Bible really is the story of God and his never-ending pursuit of relationship with his creation.

## Other Shaping Influences

Three other dramatic, shaping influences from this heritage in Enlightenment thought need to be remembered. First, alongside our new understanding of the laws of nature and the closed universe in which we live came the belief that with human reason and examination available through the five senses, humans could understand—or perhaps we should say "control"—truth in all of its forms. The result was a growing view of the material world as a machine. The same machine-like view became the standard for all aspects of human beings and human behavior. Science could and would be able to comprehend how all of the parts work. This mechanistic perspective meant tremendous gains in technology and medical insights into the human body. It also tended to treat all of life, including church, as a machine. As with any machine, then, "newer" soon became more valuable than "older." Anytime the machine wasn't running right, the "fix" was to be found in changing parts.

Second, this high view of human reason and the quest for truth through the collection of scientific data brought about the dismissal of all truth claims that could not be verified by empirical evidence (i.e., data available through the five senses). On the one hand, that meant the end of witch hunts and speculations about ghosts, demons, and vampires. Halloween became a tame evening for collecting sacks of candy for children. It also meant the demise of the "principalities and powers." For some, it meant abandoning any truth claims regarding the miraculous. Since virgins never give birth to babies in our human experience, how could one believe such a claim from millennia past? On the other hand, even those who believed God really did act in miraculous ways in the world of the Bible commonly admitted that he no longer acts in such ways today. Some openly advocated Deism, the view that God once worked in creation but had since stopped all interaction with his creation. Others, seeking to defend the stories in Scripture, too often lived as functional Deists. God's active participation in the world ceased at the time Scripture was completed and would resume again only at the Second Coming of Jesus. In the meantime, human attention to Bible study, church practice, and moral living was our responsibility. Only in the last few decades have we begun to take seriously again the belief that God is truly active in our world and in our lives.

Third, and perhaps most damaging to our consideration of church and gospel, the emphasis on the ability of the individual to think and reason for oneself led to the conviction that human identity is self-contained. While we may admit various community or family ties that name us and claim us, identity is about the self—self-esteem must be generated from within the individual, self-fulfillment must come from personal decisions implemented by the force of personal will.

Can you see the point of how that plays out in the context of proclaiming the gospel? Salvation must also be individualized. Thus, we speak about "personal relationship with God" as an

individuated event. Community identity—life in the church—
becomes an unnecessary and often untidy complication to faith.
Church is the place where Christians discover all the things
about which they disagree! Church becomes the location for
arguments about doctrine. The Good News is just about me and
God—but mostly, from the standpoint of practicality, me. What
is the inevitable outcome of such thinking? We created a way of
approaching Scripture which in the nineteenth century was the
reason for division among churches. The proliferation of denominations became, at the end of the twentieth century, reason
enough for saying, "Jesus, yes; church, no!"

### Back to the Bible

We also need to stop momentarily and think about how we
otherwise read stories and about the kind of episodes we find in
this story we call the Bible. Sometimes stories are moralized—as
if they were alternate versions of Aesop's Fables—where the
goal is to come up with a punch line at the end that tells us how
to live. Others stories are told to shock us into thinking differently; Jesus told parables that worked that way. Sometimes stories are entertaining escapes from our own realities. They may
even become fantasies that we wish we could live out. So we
need to clarify what we mean by "story" and what the goal of
this biblical story is. The best stories, we would argue, draw us
into to them so that we become vicarious participants in them.
We actually begin to see ourselves, our own stories, within those
stories. And, when we are done, we realize that we have been
changed by them.

One of the great discoveries one makes by reading the
Bible is that it is an NC-17-rated book. There are stories included in it that we don't want our children to see or hear. When it
comes to the human characters, there's nothing inhumane left
to be discussed because sooner or later humans behave in such
heinous, reviling ways in these stories. And it is precisely in the
midst of that destruction that the story of God unfolds.[12]

It begins with the beginning—creation—stated in wonderfully poetic terms in the opening chapter with the rhythmic

repetition of "And God said..." balanced by "and there was morning and evening." Finally, the earth is full of life and the ultimate earth-being is created—human, male and female, created in God's image. Paradise living is only briefly described and experienced, however, because humans are given the capacity to choose by their Creator. If they cannot choose other than to live in relationship with their Creator, after all, there cannot be true love and community. Otherwise it is all divine puppetry and only a mockery of love.

Then the crisis of sin enters the world, and humans are expelled from Paradise. The break in community with God becomes so severe that the Creator starts all over again. With the flood, creation is reduced to chaos once more. Creation is preserved, however, through the human Noah who found favor in God's sight. Yet the relationship between God and creation is once more interrupted by human efforts to become like God—in this case, through building a tower into the heavens. So the languages are confused and people are scattered to the four winds.

Then God calls Abram (for no apparent reason, cf. Gen. 12:1; Josh. 24:2f) and initiates the return of humans to community. The nation of Israel is formed and blessed by God—called to be a blessing to the nations (Exodus 19:1-6). The intent of the calling and the intent of covenant are to allow Israel to become the window to the world for humanity to experience community with God. But Israel turns inward, the call becomes exclusive rather than inclusive, and there are centuries of interaction with God in which he allows them to try human rulers, patiently endures and persists as they so often become self-absorbed to the point of idolatry, and repeatedly sends prophets with messages of warning and calls to repentance. Finally, he allows them to be destroyed and exiled as a nation, always in hopes of regaining their attention and love and loyalty.

Consider the Good News of Christ within that story. God becomes flesh and dwells among us. And it is true that one window for understanding his life and death and resurrection is that of overcoming the enemy of sin. But there are other windows. We also sing sometimes about Jesus being our Ransom. The real enemy is Satan, and the earth is Satan's dominion. God sent his son and said, "I'll give you my son in exchange for the rest of my children." Jesus was the ransom price paid to destroy the dominion of Satan. Or we sing about Jesus as the victorious conqueror who triumphed over death. In Hebrews 2, death is the enemy Jesus overcomes for us.

One image of the cross we don't think much about these days is that of Jesus as the perfect example of repentance. We humans are always double-tongued in our repentance. We say we repent, but we also have the desire to sin lurking within, making our efforts to repent less than complete. As C. S. Lewis once said, "Only a bad person needs to repent; only a good person can repent perfectly. The worse you are the more you need it and the less you can do it. The only person who could do it perfectly would be a perfect person—and he would not need it."[13] Jesus was the perfect human whose act on the cross perfectly linked repentance and forgiveness for us all.

> For those who would learn God's ways, humility is the first thing, humility is the second, and humility is the third.
>
> —Augustine of Hippo

There is also an element in the story of Jesus on the cross that models complete abandonment to God's will. When he says, "Not my will but yours be done," he makes visible the self-giving love of God. His selflessness touches those who draw near to the cross, and we partake of that selfless life. Or perhaps we could think about the cross as a new model for human behavior in which the wisdom of God confounds the wisdom of this world. The wisdom of this world believes in power and control and domination of the weak by the strong. The wisdom of God says that the greatest power is actually in weakness. God's kingdom is about sacrifice, not violence.

The point of rehearsing these other views is not to say, "Choose this one, not that one," but to get us to see how much more there is to the story. All of those views of Jesus are to be found in sacred literature. Scripture doesn't come to us with single perspectives because it is a revelation about things we could not otherwise comprehend at all. We are always going to be inadequate to the task of comprehending God or Christ or God's empowering presence in our world. The good news is that the God who created still is active in his creation. The story of God is still in process. The message of Scripture is that of an alternative worldview to the one we humans have created for ourselves.

Don't misunderstand! This is not evolution versus creation or science versus the Bible. This is not the world of human identity that must be obtained by exclusion and power, control and competition. The story of God in Scripture reveals the possibility for identity through inclusion and weakness, submission and sacrifice. It is an alternative world! It is a world in which identity is always a *we* enterprise, not *me* in isolation. It is as the collective we that the church is called to bear witness to that alternative world.

The church is where God's power is demonstrated through human weakness, where community is always inclusive, where transformation of identity comes through giving up rather than stubbornly taking hold. Yes, transformation of identity still involves victories over behaviors that are abusive to other people and to oneself. That's what sin is—the dehumanizing of oneself and/or other humans. Church is to be the community in which everyone is fully human—the widow and the orphan, rich and poor, abused and despised in this world. All find ourselves in process of being re-formed and re-created into fully human beings in the church.

Evangelism is the invitation to join the story. It is a community life to be lived, not a system of beliefs to be argued until someone relents. Those who are "in Christ" become living witnesses, evangelistic testimonies of God's ongoing story of love. This method and mode of sharing the Good News then shapes how we read Scripture and what we look for as we read together. We read the Bible to see God shaping other humans in their world in order to conform them to his image. We want to be conformed to his image in our world. How can we be that living presence now? How can we be that inclusive love of God to our world in our times? How can we be Jesus to our world as those early Christians were called to be Jesus in their world?

## Conclusion

The church is called to be a community that is always counter-intuitive to the ways of the world around us. We announce that things are not what they seem. It may appear that might makes right; it may appear that economic upward mobility is the measure of success; it may appear that it is the outward appearance that determines worth and identity; it may appear that survival of the fittest is all that matters; it may appear that consuming the natural resources of this planet is the right of whoever gets there first. But we have experienced what the Creator actually intended when he created.

There is good news for all who have been left behind by these other messages. There is good news for all who have eyes to see, ears to hear, and hearts soft enough to be touched. We open *our* stories to *your* story; we invite you to join your story with ours and discover your place in *The Story*. To live in loving community with other humans. To act in restorative ways with each other so that we may live the fully human existence God created us for in the beginning. To be the shared influences for transformation so that God by his Spirit can form us into his Holy Temple—the dwelling place of God in the midst of his creation.

### Notes

1. See the helpful discussion of the relationship of divine and human in Jesus in Jeff W. Childers and Frederick D. Aquino, *Unveiling Glory: Visions of Christ's Transforming Presence* (Abilene: ACU Press, 2003), pp. 17-56.

2. John Milbank actually traces the roots of "secular knowledge" to John Duns Scotus, a thirteenth century metaphysician who spoke of "reality as if it consisted of discrete objects, atoms, and facts." See *Theology and Social Theory: Beyond Secular Reason* (Cambridge, England: Blackwell Publishers, 1993).

3. For an indepth discussion of the impact of political and national identity on religious thought (and vice versa) in early America, see Nathan Hatch, *The Democratization of American Christianity* (New Haven: Yale University Press, 1989). He writes in the opening chapter (p. 6), "This book argues that the transitional period between 1780 and 1830 left as indelible an imprint upon the structures of American Christianity as it did upon those of American political life."

4. Mark Noll, *America's God* (New York: Oxford, 2002), p. 377.

5. For a detailed discussion, see C. Leonard Allen and Richard T. Hughes, *Discovering Our Roots: The Ancestry of Churches of Christ* (Abilene, TX: ACU Press, 1988), pp. 21-100. Also, Richard T. Hughes, *Reviving the Ancient Faith: The Story of Churches of Christ in America* (Grand Rapids: Eerdmans, 1996), pp. 26-28.

6. Campbell does preface this distinction with the comment: "That although the Scriptures of the Old and New Testaments are inseparably connected, making together but one perfect and entire revelation of the Divine will, for the edification and salvation of the Church, and therefore in that respect cannot be separated, yet as to what directly and properly belongs to their immediate object, the New Testament is as perfect a constitution...." Certainly Thomas Campbell did not intend to devalue the Old Testament, but the consequence of reading the New Testament as a "perfect constitution" could only have that long-term result.

7. See E. Brooks Holifield, *Theology in America: Christian Thought From the Age of the Puritans to the Civil War* (New Haven, CT: Yale University Press, 2003), pp. 295-96. Holifield states that Campbell expanded on the two-covenant understanding he learned in his Irish Calvinist heritage to the three dispensations of Patriarchal, Mosaic, and Christian. Campbell also believed that the Christian dispensation did not begin until the bestowing of the Spirit on Pentecost recorded in Acts. This view inevitably led to the diminishing importance of the Old Testament and the Gospels for Christian thought and practice.

8. Alexander Campbell, *The Christian System* (Cincinnati: Standard Publishing Co., 1835), p. 6.

9. Several assumptions went unquestioned in this seemingly self-evident approach to Scripture: Are the categorical methods of Aristotle foolproof? Does Aristotle's Greek methodology work well with Semitic thought? Is anyone "objective"? Can interpreters of any period divorce themselves from tradition, culture, and bias? Are ignorance and dishonesty the only possible explanations when two persons reach different conclusions from the same scriptural data? Mark Noll concludes that, with regard to the last question, there was no alternative when reason led to opposite conclusions on

the part of "reasonable people." It was this rupture of reasoning that resulted in opposing "biblical positions" on slavery and, thus, inevitable Civil War.
See the full discussion in *America's God*, pp. 377-385.

10. We are by no means the first to recognize the impact of this "fac-
tual" reading of the New Testament. Leonard Allen comes to similar conclusions when he states, "By naturalizing the Bible as a body of 'facts,' the
traditional approach atomized Scripture or broke it up into disconnected
doctrinal 'facts.' The New Testament (or at least Acts and the Epistles)
became, in practice, a field of doctrinal facts from which one could gather
almost indiscriminately. Doctrinal propositions could be assembled from
across the New Testament writings with little or no regard for historical context, for the author's intention, or for literary form and function.
'Concordance preaching' resulted—the stringing together of texts from
across the New Testament based on appearance of a single word or phrase
in the concordance." *The Cruciform Church: Becoming a Cross-Shaped
People in a Secular World* (Abilene: ACU Press, 1990), p. 33.

11. For example, speaking of the Fundamentalist movement among
Evangelicals in the early twentieth century, Robert Webber writes, "Common
Sense philosophy insisted that 'facts' could be known directly....Francis
Bacon had taught a method of analysis that consisted of gathering data, clas-
sifying it, and interpreting it. Common sense and Baconian analysis were
applied to Scripture to determine truth. The inerrant Bible as the source for
data fed into the evidential process of knowing truth. The view of inerrancy, that 'every single word of the text had been divinely inspired,' figured
prominently in the fundamentalist rejection of evolution, historical and literary criticism, and any attempt to interpret Scripture in any way other than
a literal reading of each word. Inerrancy extended to all scientific statements, to historical references, and to all numbers found in the prophecies
of future events. There was little room for symbol, poetry, or any kind of
imaginative speech." *The Younger Evangelicals: Facing the Challenges of the
New World* (Grand Rapids: Baker, 2002), p. 27.

12. In his book, *The Story We Find Ourselves In* (San Francisco: Jossey-
Bass, 2003), Brian McLaren summarizes the story of Scripture with a series
of a series of 'C' words: Creation, Crisis, Calling, Conversation, Christ,
Church, Consummation. These effectively describe the unfolding narrative
of God's redemptive love and unrelenting efforts to have relationship with
his creation.

13. C. S. Lewis, *Mere Christianity* (New York: Macmillan, 1960), p. 59.
In a section entitled "The Perfect Penitent" (pp. 56-61), Lewis states his pref-
erence for this understanding of the Atonement—while stating emphatically that no human perspective can adequately describe the event.

*Evangelism never seemed to be an "issue" in the New Testament. That is to say, one does not find the apostles urging, exhorting, scolding, planning and organizing for evangelistic programs... evangelism happened! Issuing effortlessly from the community of believers as light from the sun, it was automatic, spontaneous, continuous, contagious.*

—R. C. Halverson

# 7. OUTREACH:
# GETTING OVER OURSELVES

*For though I am free with respect to all, I have made myself a slave to all, so that I might win more of them. To the Jews I became as a Jew, in order to win Jews. To those under the law I became as one under the law (though I myself am not under the law) so that I might win those under the law. To those outside the law I became as one outside the law (though I am not free from God's law but am under Christ's law) so that I might win those outside the law. To the weak I became weak, so that I might win the weak. I have become all things to all people, that I might by all means save some.*

—1 Corinthians 9:19-22

Our fear is that the majority of Christians at the beginning of the twenty-first century see the church as a cruise ship. Ever take a vacation on one? Everybody on the ship's crew—from captain to mechanic to waiter in the dining room—is there for the comfort of the passengers. And the passengers know it. So, while being reasonably pleasant about it in most instances, they demand that things be done to their tastes, for their convenience, and with no significant exertion on their part. Cruise lines advertise for such persons and cater to their expectations. Their passengers are ultimately consumers, and the big boats must provide a delightful experience to get potential passengers to sign up. Sounds a lot like church, doesn't it? Everybody on the church staff—from ministers to maintenance crew to classroom teachers—is there for the comfort of the members. And the members know it. So, while being reasonably pleasant about it in most instances, church members want things done to their tastes, for their convenience, and with no real demands of Christian discipleship being made of them. Some churches even advertise that they are "seeker friendly"—not a bad term or bad concept, if defined properly—and cater to an appetite for "spirituality lite" that offers precious little that would make anyone radically different from their non-Christian neighbors. Their members are ultimately consumers, and they must provide a pleasant experience to get them to come, pay money for, and stay for a time.

Our conviction is that the church of God has been "dumbed down" and devalued by such an approach. The church is not a club where you pick the people you want to be with, a private school where you pay to be protected from people you don't want to be with, or a cruise ship where you have the right to demand comfort and pampering.

Does a cruise-ship mentality seem consistent with what the New Testament teaches about the community of faith called church? Does it match the statements of Jesus and his earliest followers? "If any want to become my followers, let them deny themselves and take up their cross daily and follow me," said Jesus. "For those who want to save their life will lose it, and those who lose their life for my sake will save it" (Luke 9:23-24). Does that sound like an ad for a pleasure cruise? "I have been crucified with Christ; and it is no longer I who live, but it is Christ who lives in me," wrote Paul. "And the life I now live in the flesh I live by faith in the Son of God, who loved me and gave himself for me" (Gal. 2:19b-20). Does that sound like a consumer-Christian in a comfort-zone church?

But maybe someone dismisses the statement from Jesus as

hyperbole. And the same person will surely say that Paul was a super-Christian who lived to a standard that ordinary disciples don't have the capacity—or duty—to embrace. Then what are we to make of the following text?

> You have forgotten the exhortation that addresses you as children—
>
> "My child, do not regard lightly the discipline of the Lord,
>     or lose heart when you are punished by him;
> for the Lord disciplines those whom he loves,
>     and chastises every child whom he accepts."
>
> Endure trials for the sake of discipline. God is treating you as children; for what child is there whom a parent does not discipline? If you do not have that discipline in which all children share, then you are illegitimate and not his children. Moreover, we had human parents to discipline us, and we respected them. Should we not be even more willing to be subject to the Father of spirits and live? For they disciplined us for a short time as seemed best to them, but he disciplines us for our good, in order that we may share his holiness. Now, discipline always seems painful rather than pleasant at the time, but later it yields the peaceful fruit of righteousness to those who have been trained by it (Heb. 12:5-11).

The word *disciple* has a direct relationship to the word *discipline*. We have reduced the former to make it equivalent to "church member"; we have even worked at making the latter refer principally to Bible study, prayer, and church attendance. But that trivializes Christian faith. It makes being a Christian little more than being a Republican or Democrat, being a dues-paying and attend-whenever-possible Rotarian or Civitan. Dietrich Bonhoeffer captured the spirit of the biblical texts above with his oft-quoted line about discipleship: "When Christ calls a man, he bids him come and die."[1]

For anyone who takes the Word of God seriously, the church will not be understood as a cruise ship but as a battleship. The cry that wakes us is not a gentle "Ding-dong-ding: Breakfast is being served for the next two hours" but an authoritative "All hands on deck!" In response to that call, leaders, teachers, givers, encouragers, mercy-showers, and the rest of the battle-equipped people of God report not for entertainment but to posts of duty (cf. Rom. 12:6-8). But sailors don't know how to man a battle station who have not been through boot camp and training. And that's where the church of our adult lives has failed miserably. It is also where we have failed miserably in our own ministries. And it is where corrective work must be focused immediately in most local churches—and for the foreseeable future.

> *But you will receive power when the Holy Spirit has come upon you; and you will be my witnesses in Jerusalem, in all Judea and Samaria, and to the ends of the earth.*
>
> —Acts 1:8

Before you let the battleship metaphor turn you off because of the militaristic abuses of people in the name of Christ through the centuries, both physical and verbal, some clarification might help. The enemy with whom you are to do battle as a member of Christ's blood-washed host is not some brother with whom you disagree on the interpretation of a biblical text; so long as he confesses faith in and love for Jesus as Savior and Lord, he is your brother and comrade-in-arms. Your enemy is not the drug addict, prostitute, white-collar corporate criminal, or even the person who does not confess that Jesus is the Son of God; these people are the victims of our enemy. The enemy is Satan.

"Be self-controlled and alert. Your enemy the devil prowls around like a roaring lion looking for someone to devour" (1 Pet. 5:8 NIV). Who is our enemy? The devil! And it is our call as Christ-followers to "resist" Satan and always to be "steadfast" in our faith (1 Pet. 5:9). And because he doesn't fight only in full-frontal assault, the methods by which we engage him must be varied and creative. According to Paul, Satan even disguises himself as an "angel of light" to deceive people (2 Cor. 11:14). And it is altogether possible that he has won many souls to his side in the great cosmic struggle between good and evil by showing gentle restraint over against the wild and irresponsible attacks of Christians. For example, can anyone really doubt that the wild-eyed Christian (?) fanatic who spews hate-filled slogans against abortionists, homosexuals, or Muslims drives people away from Jesus Christ? Makes it impossible for people to hear the gospel? Makes the church an object of derision?

God's work in the world will always need a certain percentage of apologists, scholars, and evangelists. These are front-line combatants who proclaim and defend the gospel. They articulate the story of Jesus in culture-appropriate language and with a readiness to explain and defend it against detractors. But we have erred in making these few into the model for the many in our churches. God needs far more foot-washers than scholars. It is far more crucial that a church be known for its compassion to the poor than for its outstanding preaching. More people will be attracted to Christ by a church whose members live Christian integrity, self-control, and joy in the workplace than by life-distanced churches that major in seminars on eschatology. It isn't that we don't need scholars, preachers, and teachers. But we have typically invested more in showcasing the few than in equipping the larger body of Christ for ministry.

## Missional Christianity

It is time for the church to take discipleship seriously. Another way of saying this is to say that we must get over ourselves; the church isn't a cruise ship that functions for the comfort and pleasure of its members—otherwise we'll book passage on another line. We must get over the worldly selfishness we have brought as baggage into the Body of Christ. We must get over the church-as-building syndrome and learn to be church-as-people-in-transformation. Only then will we be evangelistic in the way the earliest church was evangelistic. Richard Halverson was correct in pointing out that the apostles never had to do the exhorting and scolding and programming that churches do today in the name of evangelism. Among those people who remembered the presence of the Incarnate Christ in their midst, outreach with the gospel issued as effortlessly as light from the sun; evangelism really was automatic, spontaneous, continuous, and contagious for them—and must become so for us.

Paul certainly seems to envision a church that functions differently from those in which we grew up. He understood that the role of Christians gifted for leadership was *to equip and train the larger body for service.* That is, the modern clergy system in which the few perform the spiritual duties of the many was not in view with the apostle. He visualized and participated in a church the presence of the Spirit of God revolutionized families, communities, and cities. Perhaps it was to avoid fostering in the church a pagan system of faith in ceremonies performed by hired professionals (e.g., priests, oracles, clergy) that kept Paul from accepting financial support from those to whom he ministered as an apostle-teacher (cf. 1 Thess. 2:9; 1 Cor. 9:12).

The Pauline vision was that people with certain gifts from the Holy Spirit would serve the larger community by teaching and equipping it for service. "The gifts [Christ] gave were that some would be apostles, some prophets, some evangelists, some pastors and teachers, to equip the saints for the work of ministry, for building up the body of Christ, until all of us come to the unity of the faith and of the knowledge of the Son of God, to maturity, to the measure of the full stature of Christ" (Eph. 4:11-13). We see that process in terms of four stages: care, instruction, equipping, and service.

*Care.* The first thing anyone will need who has been called out of the world and called into a new community is attention and care. This calls for the church to be a loving community where there is no longer Jew or Greek, slave or free, male or female. In other words, people who are accustomed to distinctions based on gender, ethnicity, caste, wealth, education, beauty, talent, and all the other things that give status in the world must be received into and learn to experience unity in Christ. "There is no longer Jew or Greek, there is no longer slave or free, there is no longer male or female; for all of you are one in Christ Jesus" (Gal. 3:28). Other forms of care may also be needed. Some in the Jerusalem church had to be kept from poverty by the generosity of the church (Acts 4:34). New Christians at Corinth had to be nurtured, challenged, and held accountable out of the brokenness of their previous lives (1 Cor. 6:9-11).

This concept of care envisions a community of faith functioning very much as a hospital for spiritual recovery. The Great Physician has accepted John and Mary to his redemptive practice, but he employs others who are already in various stages of their own recovery process to help effect a full cure. As was pointed out in Chapter 5, church leaders would do well to study Alcoholics Anonymous for a model of something that has been lost in local churches. As a new way of life, both sobriety and Christian virtue require community in which people lovingly support one another.

*Instruction.* Once a person has been received, stabilized, and introduced to the local church as a caring community, a process of productive education can begin. By "productive education" we mean not simply Bible study but the Spirit-created and Spirit-sustained transformation of mind, heart, and lifestyle that takes place in the context of community at all levels of one's new life. There is a new worldview to learn by immersion both in the story of God found in Scripture and in the people of God who live in community. Music, prayer, and reflection on the Word of God in times of corporate worship train the novice in a new way of reading reality. What the world has been telling her for so many years has to be uprooted and replaced with the truth of God's Word. The Lord's Supper simultaneously speaks to her about the historical event of Christ's death and resurrection, renews a sense of covenant relationship with God through Christ's redemptive work, and assures her that she is now part of the living Body of Christ that is the church.

In addition to the learning that takes place in corporate worship, there will likely be classes for systematic study of the Bible that goes beyond what a sermon can do. The sermon will more nearly seek to inspire Christians to believe that the power of the

Holy Spirit is at work among them and to encourage them along the path of spiritual formation. More systematic study of the Word of God that makes the Bible a useful tool for personal growth will take place under competent teachers in smaller groups. More and more, however, people are discovering the value of small groups in homes (i.e., house churches) where quality relationships form among believers in conjunction with Bible study, prayer, and accountability.

*Equipping.* The first two stages in this process are rather obvious—though by no means easy to accomplish. We make efforts to achieve them. We lament their absence or our failure to do them as well as we would like. The third stage is largely missing in most churches of our acquaintance. How does one learn to pray? Share his faith? Teach the Bible either to young people or adults? Handle money responsibly? Parent in a way that honors God? Encourage Christians who have fallen into Satan's snare? Host and lead a house church? These are constant needs within every church, and we sometimes scold people for not being faithful in responding to them. Perhaps we are upbraiding them for something that is the fault of the leaders. Paul explicitly taught that church leaders are "to equip the saints for the work of ministry." And our "ministry" is seldom to move thousands of miles away to be a missionary. It will more often be to take a holy, peaceful, joyous, and Christ-like presence into the places where we live, study, and work. This is the ministry of salt and light to which Jesus has called us (Matt. 5:14-16).

For that matter, how effective are most churches in helping identify and nurture even the leadership gifts of a few? We seem to assume that shepherding, teaching, or administering the life of a church will happen spontaneously. Perhaps we expect companies to train people for their business and professional roles, and the church will benefit from their investment. Both assumptions are wrong. For one thing, even those persons with obvious "natural" abilities to lead need training and mentoring. For another, those who get their leadership training on a business model are not being taught to lead by Jesus' self-emptying relational model but by a bottom-line corporate model.

*Service.* The final stage in this completed process finds the discipled-and-equipped church serving people in a variety of ways. And this joyous service to the Lord produces both a positive image of the church in the minds of unbelievers and invites them to share in its life. As they respond to that invitation, the process starts over again, with the church receiving and caring for people who have been wounded by the world. In the pluralistic world of Postmodernity, it will not be particularly effective to try to argue people into embracing a set of superior beliefs or purer doctrines. What does hold promise in such a culture is visible demonstration of the transformed relationships and purer lifestyle of people who say they are following Jesus Christ. If Christianity doesn't get us off our church properties and into the needs of our larger communities, the people from those larger communities aren't going to come onto our properties for instruction in how to live.

Brian McLaren, who has written extensively on both the challenges and opportunities of the paradigm shift from Modernity to Postmodernity, makes an important point about the meaning of loving, joyous Christian service in a pluralistic culture.

> I was once talking with Dallas Willard about Islam. He dropped this little thought virus: "Remember, Brian, in a pluralistic world, a religion is valued by the benefits it brings to its non-adherents." The virus has taken hold in my thinking, bringing to mind sayings of our Lord, like "the birds of the air" nesting in the branches of the kingdom of God, people seeing the light of our good deeds and "glorifying your Father in heaven," "by their fruits you will know them."
>
> How different is this missional approach to the "rhetoric of exclusion" that worked so well in modernity: "There are blessings to being on the inside. You're on the outside and so can't enjoy them. Want to be a blessed insider like us?"
>
> In contrast, missional Christianity says, "God is expressing his love to all outsiders through our acts of

kindness and service. You're invited to leave your life of accumulation and competition and self-centeredness to join us in this mission of love, blessing, and peace. Want to join in the mission?"[2]

### "Not to Be Served But to Serve..."

Serving people as Jesus did makes you a happier, more fruitful, and more unselfish person. Serving others in the name of the Lord Jesus transforms you into a stronger Christian and gives you credibility for sharing the gospel with non-disciples. It engages you in the lifestyle for which you were made, from which sin has alienated you, and to which redemption has both called and empowered you. It identifies you as a missional Christian and becomes an invitation for others to join you in seeking after God.

The late psychiatrist Dr. Karl Menninger was once asked what a person suffering from depression should do. Dr. Menninger understood very well that depression is a complex disease process. It is often chemical in origin and can be treated very successfully with a combination of medications and therapy. Yet some of it is rooted in circumstances rather than brain physiology, and Dr. Menninger was surely addressing that segment of the population when he offered this shocking answer: "Lock up your house, go across the tracks, find someone in need, and do something to help that person."

In this narcissistic time, people can become so immersed in their own troubles that they think only of themselves. Such persons are notorious for throwing "pity parties" for themselves and inviting everyone else to come. All sorts of negative, self-defeating thoughts begin to flood—and sometimes drown—them. When the world sees an alternative to that sort of negative self-absorption, it perks up and pays attention.

Hollywood made the point that people are helped to be emotionally healthy by getting outside their confining little worlds with the movie *Patch Adams*. It's not a classic movie, by any means. It has some words and scenes we wouldn't recommend for children. But the movie makes the point that getting outside ourselves for the sake of others is an experience of healing—on both the giving and receiving end. The movie is based on the life of Dr. Hunter "Patch" Adams. He is a physician who never quite fit the mold of his profession. He was officially criticized in his medical school record for "excessive happiness" and was told by a faculty adviser, "If you want to be a clown, join the circus."

The real Dr. Adams wears bright floral shirts rather than a white coat. He is not above dressing in a gorilla suit or filling a room with balloons to get his patients to smile. He founded an unorthodox clinic called the Gesundheit Institute after graduating from medical school. When it generated a lot of media coverage in the 1980s, he wrote a book about his work in 1993. The movie is based on that book.

Dr. Adams was inspired to go into medicine by an experience he had while a patient in a psychiatric ward when he was eighteen years old. Adams' fellow patient, Rudy, imagined that vicious squirrels were threatening him. It occurred to the teen-ager to help Rudy conquer his fears by inventing a game. That event is chronicled in the movie, and it is hilarious as played by Robin Williams. Says the real Patch Adams:

> *We must know people—like them, enjoy them, make friends with them, take trouble for them—before it may ever be right to "speak" to them about spiritual matters.*
>
> —Samuel M. Shoemaker

No friends came to visit Rudy; I had lots of visitors. His tears weighed a million pounds, while mine barely had the weight to drop to the ground. When I was caring about Rudy I was no longer suffering; it took my mind off my own troubles and I became embarrassed about my pain compared to his. The experience helped me discover what a jubilant thrill it is to help others.[3]

It is easy for Christians to figure out why the underlying thesis of joy through self-emptying rings true from the movie. It is the way of life modeled for us by Jesus. And it is the path he wants his disciples to travel. In response to an argument among his disciples about position and prestige in the kingdom of heaven, he told them, "Whoever wishes to be great among you must be your servant, and whoever wishes to be first among you must be your slave; just as the Son of Man came not to be served but to serve, and to give his life a ransom for many" (Matt. 20:26b-28).

Jesus came to save us from the clutches of Satan and the power of sin. One of the ways you know you are beginning to get stronger in your spiritual life is that you find yourself getting beyond spiritual infancy. You no longer have to be carried, coddled, and cuddled all the time. You actually find yourself helping others and carrying their burdens. Spiritual immaturity is always complaining that people aren't doing enough for me—they're not noticing me, not inviting me, not asking me to participate. And all of us have been at that point of immaturity. Spiritual maturity is evidenced by people who serve others without concern for being noticed, applauded, or rewarded.

In our own home church, we are blessed to know and draw on the credibility of so many people who serve others unselfishly. We make our building—which was constructed to be flexible in function—available to Metro Public Schools, private schools, and neighborhood groups. A variety of twelve-step programs meet on the property every week. Little Red School House starts hundreds of kids off to school in the fall with supplies they would not have had otherwise because of their parents' poverty or lack of concern. Second Saturday Ladies minister to families in the ICU waiting rooms at Vanderbilt Hospital. Compassion is the principal spiritual gift of the people God has drawn to our church family, and it is humbling to see so many people using that blessed gift constantly.

The boldest and most comprehensive project of service we've had the faith to dream yet at Woodmont Hills is a partnership with Schrader Lane Church of Christ and is called Christian Community Services, Inc. It is a ministry designed to empower low-income families to a level of economic, social, and personal independence. Founded in 1997, CCSI is a family mentoring program that has already allowed many families to get off all public assistance and to be economically self-sufficient. There are seven people who can be pointed to at the date of our writing this book who have not only gotten off welfare but who have become homeowners.

It is incredibly humbling to hear someone like Pamela Gant tell the story of her fight to overcome addiction to crack cocaine, to make a life for her two children, and to break a poverty cycle she had once accepted as her fate—and to hear her give the glory to God for showing her that life could be lived differently than she had ever known. As Pamela tells her story, she relates how she never wanted to be on welfare. So she prayed a simple prayer: "Help! Jesus, please help me!" And God answered her prayer by allowing a Christian family to mentor her, help her learn to budget her money, and become a better mother to her daughter and son. Government agencies had made resources and programs available to her; CCSI put people who saw her with the eyes of Jesus into her life, people who cared about Pam as a woman in God's image rather than as a case number. It's amazing how people respond to love and respect.

If churches could ever manage to *get over ourselves* (i.e., shift from a cruise-ship mentality) and *get outside ourselves* (i.e., give meaningful, joyous service to the victims of their enemy), the result would be missional Christians. For clarity's sake, a missional Christian is one who has passed through the four-stage process already described and who is now representing Jesus faithfully in the places where he or she has influence.

We're not talking about missionary recruitment for foreign countries. What we envision instead is a local church whose mindset has embraced such a kingdom vision for itself that its members are authentic light, salt, and leaven in a community. A missional Christian is a manager or executive who sees her task as representing Jesus to the people she leads; she is a competent professional who does her work with excellence, but her primary self-image is to bring a taste of the kingdom of God to those with whom she works. He is a salesman who is prompt, enthusiastic, thorough, and ethical, but he is more interested in bearing the image of God faithfully than in getting rich. It is the kindergarten, seventh-grade, or graduate school teacher who not only communicates needed information in effective ways but also treats students and fellow-teachers, bus drivers and maintenance workers with dignity, respect, and love.

These missional Christians don't make points within a church system or within some legalistic interpretation of Scripture for setting up Bible studies or leading people to professions of faith. They are simply being authentic citizens of the kingdom of God. The all-hands-on-deck mentality of a battleship church has helped them see that Christ needs someone representing him in every place the members of that church are scattered throughout a community during the week—in offices, at medical clinics, in classrooms, during family outings to the beach, when someone's car has broken down, or after a tragic death in the family three doors down the street.

Scotty Smith, senior pastor of the nearby Christ Community Church in Franklin, Tennessee, talks about "God's people in God's places doing God's things under God's reign." That's an excellent working definition of missional Christians. And God has put the vast majority of his people not on paid church staffs but in the workaday world of real life. The task of church staffs must be seen increasingly in terms of training and equipping the larger multitude of the body of Christ to function in the places where God has put them. Wouldn't that be a more effective strategy than one which has the larger body of a local church looking to its handful of paid staff members to take a neighborhood or city for Christ?

J.I. Packer uses this metaphor to drive home the Pauline truth that the church is like a human body in which every single part has a function to supply:

> The church is not to be like a bus, where passengers sit quietly and let someone else do the driving, but like an anthill, where everybody is at work. Not everyone who

thus ministers will be a church officer, nor will the service they render always be appreciated. But just as every bit of that fabulous complex, the human body, has a job to do, so it is with each of us who believe.[4]

The church as embodied in local congregations of believers is a laboratory for the kingdom of heaven on Planet Earth. The self-image of every local church need to be that it is a microcosm of the kingdom of heaven to its surrounding community. The world is under the dominion of the Prince of Darkness and has not yielded allegiance to the Son of God. In our response to the gospel, Christians have been called out of the world and into Christ's spiritual body. We have been washed, sanctified, and dressed in righteousness to be his lovely bride. Our task now is to learn the thinking and behavior appropriate to our new citizenship. We are "*in* the world" but determined not to be "of the world" for his sake. So we assemble, tell the story of our Savior, and participate in community-formation events such as worship, baptism, the Lord's Supper, and fellowship. But we depart those assemblies inspired to be representatives of Christ to everyone with whom we interact—from the taxi driver to the food server to the teenager making change at the grocery store.

As we learn the rhythms of this new way to live, we experience eternal life. Eternal life, after all, is not what we get as a reward for being Christians after we die. It is the new, Spirit-empowered lifestyle that happens among the people of God here and now. The full blossoming of that life awaits the return of Christ, but it has begun already—if it is authentic. Transformed by the Spirit's power and growing through our sometimes-bumpy interactions with one another—cushioned by love, patience, and discipline from more mature Christians—we are tasting the kingdom of God. We are experiencing his sovereign rule over our intellects, emotions, and behaviors. Onlookers are drawn to such a community as moths to a flame. In all the places where that church has members, its influence is being felt. Its outreach is being extended. Its evangelistic strategy of beauty and joy is being implemented.

### Staggering Needs

When you see the staggering needs of a world that is spiritually dead, it is easy to feel overwhelmed and to be paralyzed. God certainly doesn't expect you to help everybody in need. He doesn't even expect your church to help everyone who is in trouble. That would be too heavy a burden. It is a burden even Jesus couldn't shoulder during his own personal ministry. So what are we supposed to do in the face of overwhelming poverty and drug or alcohol addiction? How are we supposed to respond to unemployment and dysfunctional families? How can we be God's instruments for hope among the hopeless?

> *To earn the right to speak words of love, we must first willingly demonstrate deeds of love with the hurting people of our cities.*
>
> —Steve Sjogren

An article appeared several years ago in *Time* magazine about a physician who lived through the terrible bombing of Hiroshima. When the blast hit, Dr. Fumio Shigeto was waiting for a streetcar about a mile from the city's center. At that distance, he was sheltered from the force of the blast by the corner of a concrete building. He began hearing the screams of victims almost immediately. Not knowing what had happened, he stood there bewildered and overwhelmed. He was only one doctor wondering how he could respond to a city filled with desperately ill patients. Dr. Shigeto knelt, opened his black bag, and began treating the person lying at his feet.

Dr. Shigeto's experience is our own. Having survived alcoholism or divorce, toxic church life or childhood abuse, what is your ministry? Having been delivered from prostitution or homosexuality, whom can you serve? Having found a way to put your life together after cancer, a divorce, or a job loss, where should you focus your ministry? Serve someone near you! Reach to someone whose situation you understand and who can believe you care about her or him!

*There is a tricky thing about serving others in Jesus' name: You must serve people as he did—without expectations, without steamrolling their personhood or responsibility, and without abandoning God's primary call on your own life.* It is possible to help too much. And it is possible to think we are helping by making people dependent on us rather than empowering them for the life to which God is calling them.

Here is a critical text on this point: "Bear one another's burdens, and in this way you will fulfill the law of Christ. For if those who are nothing think they are something, they deceive themselves. All must test their own work; then that work, rather than their neighbor's work, will become a cause for pride. For all must carry their own loads" (Gal. 6:2-5).

First, this text teaches us to "bear one another's burdens" without wresting from those strugglers the responsibility to "carry their own loads." Today we use terms like "setting limits" or "establishing boundaries" with other human beings. Compassion must not cross the line into taking over another person's life or trying to control that person. Neither should compassion be understood as refusing to say "No" when the person you are trying to help doesn't follow through or tries to take advantage of your generosity of intent and action. If you allow people to view you as the expert or their problem-solver, you may be helping for your own sake rather then theirs. Needing to be needed is a snare that true servants avoid.

Second, it requires us to respect the freedom and integrity of others. People who participate in CCSI, for example, don't have to attend church. They don't have to become Christians or enroll their children in Sunday School to need and deserve our assistance. Compassion may lead to an opportunity to share the gospel, but Jesus helped people simply because he loved them and honored them. Loving someone enough to be helpful must not be a means to an end but as an end in itself. Having said that, however, we would hasten to add that joyous service from a loving heart is often the means of drawing someone's favorable attention to Christ. In fact, it is by getting outside ourselves that we begin to look like Christ, draw people into the biblical narrative, and provide them a way to link their life stories to God's story.

## A Story That Isn't Safe

Some of the most effective evangelists we have ever known had no idea they were evangelizing anyone. They were simply going about the business of living their faith in Jesus Christ with such integrity that it caused someone to question their negative, pejorative image of Christians and churches, to begin a personal quest for authentic meaning for life, and eventually to discover that Jesus Christ is the Way, the Truth, and the Life. And that is how people in Postmodern times will be reached—not by argument but by authenticity, not by logic but by love. So perhaps it is time that we quit thinking of spiritual outreach as mugging missions into enemy territory with Bibles, tracts, and memorized answers to questions and start seeing it instead as *a process of engaging people with the story of Jesus.*

At the start of the movie *The Neverending Story,* a boy named Bastian is running away from some other kids. He ducks into a bookstore to hide and is challenged by the owner. The old man says something to the effect that the boy doesn't belong in his store because he isn't a reader. Protesting that he does indeed read books, a conversation follows about books that tell "safe" stories—stories you read as fiction or for their historical information, put down, and walk away from—and a "special" book that is altogether different from the rest.

> "What's that book about?" asks Bastian.
> "Oh, this is something *special,*" says the bookstore owner.
> "Well, what is it?"
> "Look, your books are safe," the owner says. "By reading them you get to become Tarzan or Robinson Crusoe."
> "But that's what I like about them," replies Bastian.
> "Ah, but afterwards you get to be a little boy again."

"What do you mean?" asks Bastian.

"Listen," says the man. "Have you ever been Captain Nemo, trapped inside your submarine while the giant squid is attacking you?"

"Yes," says Bastian.

"Weren't you afraid you couldn't escape?"

"But it's only a *story!*"

"That's what I'm talking about," says the man. "The ones you read are safe."

"And this one isn't?"[5]

The Bible *isn't* safe! It *isn't* one of those books to be read merely for the stories of Noah's Ark, Joseph's Coat, and Jesus' kindness to children. It is the narrative account of God's purpose to redeem sinful-but-dearly-loved humanity through his grace that has been revealed in Jesus Christ. And people who overhear or see a visual image of that story are inclined to want to get into the narrative and follow through with their own involvement in that unique story.

Let us say it another way: Your story is our story is the story of every human life, and our personal and collective stories make sense only in relation to *God's* story as narrated and modeled for us by Jesus Christ. The gospel is not a series of doctrinal affirmations over which to battle. It is the unfolding story in human history of God's purpose for the creatures he made in his own image and likeness.

If evangelism is drawing people into the story of Jesus—challenging people to see themselves and all the events and relationships of their lives in light of a personal relationship with Jesus as their way, truth, and life—how do we share his story with them? How do we invite them to channel the streams and tributaries of their human experience into the ocean vastness of God's love for them in Christ? How do we call them to find meaning, identity, and purpose in him?

This is the perennial challenge to Christ's church—to draw people into the Jesus narrative. It doesn't change in the face of Modernity or Postmodernity, socialism or capitalism, pre-9/11 or post-9/11, wealth or poverty. Cultural movements always offer the option of shutting out God, pursuing a self-willed agenda, and suffering the inevitable consequences. Paul described one of those historical epochs in an epistle he wrote in the seventh decade of the first Christian century.

> And so I insist—and God backs me up on this—that there be no going along with the crowd, the empty-headed, mindless crowd. They've refused for so long to deal with God that they've lost touch not only with God but with reality itself. They can't think straight anymore. Feeling no pain, they let themselves go in sexual obsession, addicted to every sort of perversion (Eph. 4:17-19, *The Message*; cf. Rom. 1:18ff).

Sounds strangely familiar, doesn't it? People have lost touch not only with God but with reality itself! They don't think straight. And what is the Christian alternative to that upside-down world? How do we reach the people who have let themselves go in behaviors such as sexual obsession and addiction?

> But that's no life for you. You've learned Christ! My assumption is that you have paid careful attention to him, been well instructed in the truth precisely as we have it in Jesus. Since, then, we do not have the excuse of ignorance, everything—and I do mean everything—connected with that old way of life has to go. It's rotten through and through. Get rid of it! And then take on an entirely new way of life—a God-fashioned life, a life renewed from the inside and working itself into your conduct as God accurately reproduces his character in you (Eph. 4:20-24, *The Message*).

People who have been cared for by the church and instructed in the way of Christ model an alternative worldview for their neighbors. We have given up on the old way of life that is rotten to the core and started on a spiritual adventure leading to an entirely new way of life. It is life renewed from the inside (by the Holy Spirit) and life that shows itself more and more as a God-fashioned life. It is life that shows not contempt but compassion for people caught in the world's undertow—knowing that they are not our enemies but victims of our enemy. Equipped now with new skills that bless people and allow them to sense the presence of Jesus, it is life that gives unselfishly and serves joyously. And that life is the best answer to Modernity's theoretical, linear, process-oriented, and standardized cynicism, to Postmodernity's practical, experiential, chaotic, outcomes-oriented, and individualized skepticism, or to any other cultural option to the Christian faith.

> *Nothing can happen through you which is not happening to you.*
>
> —Lloyd John Ogilvie

Our neighbors won't get caught up in the story of Jesus until they see us authentically caught up in it. The key to evangelism is not bumper stickers, T-shirts, and tracts. It is *bona fide* imitation of Jesus. When our churches are cultural alternatives to the world's racism and sexism, jealousy and rivalry, selfishness and materialism, then and only then will we be light in a dark world. And it must be not just your church but you as that person's neighbor—a person who keeps promises, lives with integrity, cares about others, and demonstrates an appealing, joyous way of life. Then they will open up to you about their emptiness and confusion. They will want to know more about your beliefs and life commitments. They will be open to talking about Jesus with you, coming to church events with you, reading a piece of literature that tells the basics of Christian faith, or joining your small-group Bible study. In the process of interacting with the community of faith, they can embrace faith and be saved. They can be encountered by the Holy Spirit and transformed.

### Conclusion

Before we have the right to say anything *about* Jesus to people, we are called to *be* Jesus to them. Our Bible verses or invitation to church assemblies have no serious weight apart from our God-fashioned lives. Our own personal life stories must be one with the biblical narrative of God's love that has been enfleshed in Jesus. Something must be noticeably different or at least in the process of transformation before we can have real credibility to talk about Jesus to the non-Christian men and women around us.

That doesn't mean you have to have everything figured out. You don't have to be perfect. You don't have to have it all together. But you do have to have a clear direction, a definite purpose for your existence on Planet Earth. You must know who you are, whose you are, and why you are here. You must know that something has gone terribly wrong because of human sin. You must know and believe that the solution to that problem is found only in Jesus.

Evangelism as a spiritual gift (cf. Eph. 4:11) is not given to every believer. Some of us are better at telling the story with words than others. But all of us are called to be witnesses to the power of the gospel story to redeem, transform, and give meaning to life. Without the credibility of a joint witness as a congregation and your personal integrity with the person in your workplace, there is little hope that the people who know your church's meeting times and ministries or who deal with you as their neighbor will come to know Christ.

Do you understand now why we define evangelism as "a process of engaging people with the story of Jesus"? It isn't hurling Bible texts at people or winning arguments with them. It is showing them such a beautiful representation of Jesus that they are captivated by it, want to know more about the community gathered around him, want to know what is going on in the life of his bride. It is welcoming those people into our midst and inviting them to be part of our spiritual journey. It is asking them to join us in linking our personal stories with Jesus' never-ending story of redemption.

From Genesis to the Gospels to Revelation, from sin to promise to Calvary to heaven—it is the story unlike any other. You can't simply read it and put it aside. And it is not a safe story, for it will call for your personal participation in the drama. Our business as the church is to give people glimpses of Jesus by coming alongside them in the gentle way of the Son of God and serving them with joy. The beauty of his bride will let the people who are not yet disciples understand that they are being called into the holy drama themselves. And when they come, he will save them.

## Notes

1. Dietrich Bonhoeffer, *The Cost of Discipleship*, trans. Chr. Kaiser Verlag München (New York: Macmillan, 1963), p. 99.

2. Brian D. McLaren, "Emerging Values," *Leadership* 24 (Summer 2003), p. 39.

3. Patch Adams as quoted in production notes on the movie based on his life and produced by Universal Studios in 1999. Internet. Available from http://www.patchadams.com/productionmain4.html; accessed 22 December 2003.

4. J.I. Packer, "Experiencing God's Presents," *Christianity Today*, August 2003, p. 55.

5. Dialogue taken from the screenplay of *The Neverending Story* and quoted in J. Richard Middleton and Brian J. Walsh, *Truth Is Stranger Than It Used to Be* (Downers Grove, IL: InterVarsity Press, 1995), p. 195.

The gift of the Holy Spirit closes the gap between the life of God and ours. When we allow the love of God to move in us, we can no longer distinguish ours and his; he becomes us, he lives in us. It is the first fruits of the Spirit, the beginning of our being made divine.

—Austin Farrer

# 8. THE SPIRIT'S TEMPLE

*We know that the whole creation has been groaning in
labor pains until now; and not only the creation, but we
ourselves, who have the first fruits of the Spirit, groan
inwardly while we wait for adoption, the redemption of
our bodies. For in hope we were saved. Now hope that is
seen is not hope. For who hopes for what is seen? But if we
hope for what we do not see, we wait for it with patience.*
—Romans 8:22-25

Drive through practically any residential area of any city in
the United States on Sunday morning and you will see lots
of cars being washed, hear lots of lawnmowers humming, and
have to be careful of lots of children playing in or near the
streets. In other words, if you live with the assumption that
Sunday morning empties residential neighborhoods into church
buildings from 9 o'clock until noon, you are mistaken. For all the
people who are in a house of worship during that time, there
are many times more who are installing garage doors, riding
bikes, or just sleeping in. Some churches that are big on outreach and evangelism actually cruise neighborhoods near their

properties on Sunday mornings to identify unchurched people for later contact. Thus they don't "waste time" inviting people to their assemblies or informing them of the services they offer only to find out that they are members of another church a few blocks away. They focus on the growing percentage of people who have opted out of church altogether.

If you think this is an urban phenomenon rather than one that affects small-town U.S.A. and rural areas, get in your car and drive around one of those places. You'll see the same thing going on there. More and more people who once either attended a church service on Sunday morning or felt guilty for not doing so are staying home with no sense of guilt for doing so. And since church attendance is one of the minimal indicators for a Christian life, it is probably not a quantum leap to suspect that these unchurched people aren't spending a lot of their free time reading the Bible, sorting out theology, or having family devotionals.

Why are so many churches in serious decline? Why is the median age of church members across America rising? Why do so many people say the church is either irrelevant to life or a negative force in their experience? We're hardly qualified to speak to questions like these at a statistical or sociological level. But here is what George Barna says:

> Frankly, the local church in the U.S. has come on hard times. Not financially—it reaps more than ever—but in terms of its image and influence. To understand how the church could lose its edge during a time when interest in spirituality is breaking records, while people are spending literally billions of dollars on faith-related products, and seminaries are experiencing record-breaking enrollments, you have to look at the bigger picture.... In spite of the nation's population increase and a climate of rising interest in spirituality, Christian churches actually decreased in size during the '90s. They went from an average of 99 adults attending on an average Sunday in 1990 to 90 adults present on a Sunday in 2000. The reasons for the shrinkage include

the opening of several thousand new churches (which often start out with fewer people than the average existing church has); an increase in the number of unchurched adults; and the decreased frequency of attendance among churchgoers. Claims of prolific church growth have been grossly exaggerated; not only are most churches not increasing in size, but those that are expanding are doing so at the expense of other churches. More than 80 percent of the adults who get counted as new adherents and thus as part of the growth statistic are really just transplants from other churches—religious consumers in search of the perfect, or at least more exciting or enjoyable, church experience. Disturbingly little church growth is attributable to new converts. All in all, [the final decade of the twentieth century] was not a good decade for church growth.[1]

Maybe a lot of what is going on simply reflects the spirit of our time. A Postmodern mindset is highly relativistic; it is not inclined to embrace Christ over Buddha or Mohammed. It is big on diversity and multiculturalism; it will be inclined to give equal weight to every point of view and defend them all as equally right and equally wrong. At the same time, there is surely a great deal of anger and resentment over the exploitation of people in the name of the church—from Roman Catholic priests abusing children to Protestant clergy building little fiefdoms of power to freelance televangelists bilking people of their life savings.

## Seeing from a Certain Point of View
It isn't that the people who are rejecting church are all atheists. Many of them would even resent being called "irreligious"—while quickly admitting to being "unchurched." A man who is active in a Baptist Church on the West Coast nevertheless admits, "I totally understand my friends who hate church or think it's boring or react negatively because of the formalities and customs. They think it's strange, stuffy, weird, and ritualistic." So we're presented with the dilemma that creates the question

around which this book has been written: *Can our churches be liberated from institutional faith and recapture the relational experience of a Christ-formed community?* Saved from ineffectiveness? Rescued from irrelevance? Delivered from death by suicide? On the one hand, we have this glorious biblical image of the church as the Bride of Christ; on the other, we confront a host of negative impressions in contemporary culture. But wait! Maybe we are only seeing in the bride a phenomenon we witnessed earlier in the groom.

The problem may well rest with the lenses through which we see both the church and Jesus. All too often even those of us inside the church continue to see the world (and Jesus) from a strictly human point of view. We are much like Paul's declaration to the Corinthians when he says, "From now on, therefore, we regard no one from a human point of view; even though we once knew Christ from a human point of view, we know him no longer in that way" (2 Cor. 5:16). To know Christ only from a human point of view was to miss his divine identity. Saul the persecutor of the church only saw an imposter leading people away from the true faith (i.e., Judaism). His encounter on the Damascus Road was both physically blinding and spiritually eye-opening (Acts 9). He came away from that event with a radically different vision of Jesus. He experienced him as the resurrected Son of God and received the transfusion of Holy Spirit presence and Christ identity (Acts 9:17).

The Spirit's presence allowed him to see himself and the rest of humanity in a whole new way. Again, he writes to the Corinthians, "Now the Lord is the Spirit, and where the Spirit of the Lord is, there is freedom. And all of us, with unveiled faces, seeing the glory of the Lord as though reflected in a mirror, are being transformed into the same image from one degree of glory to another; for this comes from the Lord, the Spirit" (2 Cor. 3:17-18).

In our modern world, we believed for too long that it was by our physical senses that we could rationally and logically understand all knowledge and truth. It was the pursuit of "the facts" of the Bible that led us to true knowledge about God and

Jesus, and, yes, the church. So we read the stories about God in Scripture, and we read the story of Jesus in the New Testament; we even developed apologetic proofs for the rational truth of the Incarnation—the divine becoming human in the birth of Jesus. But just how "rational" can Incarnation be? While our human experiences told us that virgins don't have babies, we searched for the logic that would allow us to believe that, in the unique case of Mary, the Bible story was true. A virgin did conceive; Jesus was born of the Holy Spirit. He was human and divine—Son of Man and Son of God.

But then we struggled with that concept because we live in an "either-or world." Could our struggle relate to the fact that we were trying to make a *supra-rational* truth into a near-mundane rational fact? Were we fighting so hard against the interpretations of Christianity as *ir*-rational that we came down in the wrong place ourselves? Our empirical vision of reality continually stumbled over the claim that Jesus was fully human and fully divine. The either-or of rational-irrational must sometimes give way to a new sort of truth that is supra-rational—that is, a category of truth that is simply above and beyond what our tiny intelligences working within our limited categories can fathom.

> *Watches, cars, and Christians can all look chromed and shiny. But watches don't tick, cars don't go, and Christians don't make a difference without insides. For a Christian, that's the Holy Spirit.*
>
> —Tim Downs

It is difficult for most of us to picture Jesus as a fifteen-year-old boy with pimples. We don't spend much time thinking about Jesus going through puberty like other human males. We just assent to the claims of his sinlessness and move on to the divine declarations of his identity that accompany his baptism and the coming of the Holy Spirit "to fulfill all righteousness" (Matt. 3:15-

17; cf. Mark 1:9-11; Luke 3:21ff). Only at the cross, when he cries out "My God, My God, why have you forsaken me?" (Matt. 27:46; cf. Mark 15:33-39; Luke 23:44-48; Psa. 22:2) or perhaps in the Garden of Gethsemane when he is so distressed and prays that this cup (i.e., his death) might pass from him (Matt. 26:36-46; cf. Mark 14:32-42; Luke 22:40-46) do we allow ourselves to speak of his actual humanity. Strangely enough, however, perhaps it is at those moments we should be thinking about his divinity.

The birth of Jesus itself presents us with the mystery of human and divine becoming one entity. That mystery is further defined—and yet not really—at his baptism when the Spirit descends and the voice from heaven speaks. We are given glimpses of the mystery throughout his life as he encounters other humans—sometimes miraculously curing the diseased, amazingly feeding thousands with a sack lunch, authoritatively offering forgiveness of sins to strangers and outcasts. "Who is this who claims to forgive sins?" was the haunting question of the religiously devout who witnessed those events.

What has any of this to do at all with what people living in the twenty-first century—including us church insiders—see and think when we talk about all that's wrong with the church? Just this: The people who in Jesus' own day only saw Jesus the human could not experience the power and presence of his divinity (see especially Mark 6:1-6). To see only the human Jesus—or to see only the divine Jesus—is to not see the real Jesus at all. We suggest the same is true for all who have identified themselves with Christ and become members of his body, the church.

## Quenching the Spirit

Because we have not spent enough effort contemplating the mystery and complexity of Jesus as both human and divine, we have been equally unable to grasp the idea of our own identity in Christ as both human and divine. Whether we use the metaphor Bride of Christ or Body of Christ, there is a divine dimension of the church that is a declaration of the Spirit's presence within. The Spirit dwells within us! When we see only the human dimension of our identity, we act out of that human identity only. And then we become self-fulfilling prophecies of humanity still unable to live the life we've been invited to share. Though promised the identity of Christ and offered the example in Jesus of human existence as God intended it from the beginning, we continue to live out only the human identity without God-presence, without Spirit-indwelling. To use Paul's words again, we "quench the Spirit."

The transforming power at work in the world through the church is the God-presence of the Holy Spirit. Just as the mystery of fully human and fully divine identity was the reality of Jesus, it was and is to be the reality of the church. Yes, it is clear that early Christians also struggled to understand and embrace that transformation of identity and often failed to live up to the calling. It is even more difficult for us to embrace the identity and calling when our rational, logical lenses for acknowledging truth are so resistant to the mystery and ambiguity of such claims about divine presence and identity "in Christ." The world sees only the human weaknesses and frailties of church because the church itself most often exhibits only the human identity and weaknesses. We fail ourselves by not embracing the divine identity that transfuses and transforms us—just as it did early Christians. We need to see "no longer from a human point of view" so that we can offer a vision of the divine to the world.

Paul spent considerable space in the New Testament letters he wrote puzzling over these tensions between human and divine, faith as daily life and faith as kingdom ideal, church of God and kingdom of God. And the terms he most often used were *flesh* and *Spirit.*

"Flesh" isn't so much skin, bone, and Planet Earth as it is the frustrated created order in its struggle with and bondage to sin; "Spirit" isn't so much invisible, ghostly, and other-than-bodily as it is orientation toward and surrender to God. And when Paul writes of the tension between flesh and Spirit in the experience of the church, he is struggling in his own time and place with what we are trying to figure out in ours. How can faith seem so impotent in God's people? How can the church be so racked with heresy and immorality? How can the intentions of God for life in this world seem so close to utter and abject failure? Paul's answer must become ours: There is a great cosmic struggle going on, and the church is caught in the tension between competing powers. We are not exempt from it but wear the uniform and run the plays of our Captain Jesus. His Satanic Majesty is playing defense against you, and you will be tackled, bruised, and thrown for losses. But the game plan is sound, and—truth be told—the outcome is rigged and foretold! You will win, so long as you stay on the playing field!

> I consider that the sufferings of this present time are not worth comparing with the glory about to be revealed to us. For the creation waits with eager longing for the revealing of the children of God; for the creation was subjected to futility, not of its own will but by the will of the one who subjected it, in hope that the creation itself will be set free from its bondage to decay and will obtain the freedom of the glory of the children of God (Rom. 8:18-21).

> *Every time we say "I believe in the Holy Spirit" we mean that we believe there is a living God able and willing to enter human personality and change it.*
>
> —J.B. Phillips

Paul believed that everything in the church's present arena of operation (i.e., the created world in bondage to decay) is experiencing a sense of "futility." The present circumstances of our operation force us to feel the stress of life that is subject to weakness, stress, failure, and frustration. But those who believe the promises of God and struggle against those forces in hope are destined to experience the ultimate freedom and glory that have been vouchsafed to us by the resurrection of Jesus Christ.

We could not survive a struggle of such cosmic proportions in our own strength. That is why the individual bodies of saved men and women have been marked for God's ownership and are being given daily power for our struggle by the indwelling Spirit of God (1 Cor. 6:19). This means, in turn, that the church is the temple of God's presence in the world. "Do you not know that you are God's temple and that God's Spirit dwells in you?" (1 Cor. 3:16). This rhetorical question was put to a church beset by internal quarreling, sexual immorality, widespread spiritual immaturity, confusion about the Lord's Supper, and a host of other problems. Wouldn't you change churches if all those things were going on in yours? If it was the only church in town, wouldn't you feel compelled to plant a new one? Paul was distressed over their problems but clearly not surprised! He still considered those people "the church of God at Corinth" and counted the members of that body as "those who are sanctified in Christ Jesus, called to be saints" in service to Almighty God (1 Cor. 1:2).

Their faith in and love for Jesus Christ had set them apart from the rest of the population at Corinth. Their baptism in Jesus' name had constituted, among other things, a formal commitment to follow him and had made them components of Christ's bridal companion in that city. So established, the Holy Spirit—not only more powerful than these people who had embraced a heavenly calling but stronger than all the forces that ever could be unleashed against them—was at work among them to achieve God's holy ends among a terribly inadequate group of Corinthian disciples. They were struggling with ego and the desire to be noticed, alcoholism and homosexuality, divorce and blended families, financial crises and sickness—the very same things with which we are struggling in our congregations. If some in Corinth were inclined to despair, Paul believed they could endure by the power of the Holy Spirit at work among them.

We know that the whole creation has been groaning in labor pains until now; and not only the creation, but we ourselves, who have the first fruits of the Spirit, groan

inwardly while we wait for adoption, the redemption of
our bodies. For in hope we were saved. Now hope that
is seen is not hope. For who hopes for what is seen?
(Rom. 8:22-25).

Do you hear the apostle saying that not only the created
world generally but "we ourselves"—Christians "who have the
first fruits of the Spirit"—are waiting, hoping, and groaning as we
await creation's release from its captivity and futility? Do you not
understand that our frustrations over how to "do church" and
keep it from self-destruction are the very same ones with which
Paul dealt constantly in his first-century experience? Our time in
history is not unique. This is usual-and-customary fare for the
people of God in every historical period between the "already"
of atonement validated by the resurrection of Jesus from the
dead and the "not yet" of our own. It is what we should expect
between the "already" of a deposit of God's Spirit in us and the
"not yet" of the full blossoming of the glory we will share at
Christ's return.

In the meanwhile, we wait. While we wait, we hope. As we
live in hope, we persevere, grow, and experience gradual transformation in likeness to Christ. Interest in the seductions of this
world's environment narrow over time, and concern for the
things of God broadens. To use the words of Austin Farrer, the
gentle presence of the indwelling Holy Spirit "closes the gap
between the life of God and ours." The fruit of the Spirit begins
to bud, grow, and ripen in our lives. We begin to notice that we
are less and less controlled by what is happening on the outside
of us and more and more by the Spirit's presence inside us. And
the most obvious-to-everyone proof that something genuine is
happening in our midst is love. A body of people is being transformed into a community of love.

## The Community of Love

Much more is at stake here than a church having a benevo-
lence program or a series of twelve-step groups. While not
excluding those programmatic responses to need, the communi-

ty of love that bears witness to the Spirit's transformation is a community that literally wears the loving embrace of God. It is a perpetual state of being that exists by the Spirit's presence and power at work through individuals who have discovered the power of bodily identity in Christ. It is a recognition of life lived in imitation of Christ. As the real body of Christ, we are God's incarnation of love to one another and to the world.

While that sounds obvious and older than the oldest songs about love in our hymnbooks—and are at least as familiar to us as the words "They will know we are Christians by our love, by our love"—we believe that the transformation of the church into a community of love is exactly what the world has not yet witnessed in us. So often church continues to be experienced as discriminating, racially and socio-economically divided and dividing, or offering a message that tends to equate being Christian with being a financially successful American.

An additional tension from our own cultural environment has been the individualism and pursuit of personal spiritual identity as though we have either spirituality or identity in isolation from other people and our surrounding environment. Thus, we came to speak of personal salvation apart from the church. Individuals needed to be saved and then choose the church of their choice. Even distinctively Christian practices within worship, such as partaking of the Lord's Supper—ironically called "communion"—became best practiced and understood as an individual moment of reflection about personal salvation.

But there are signs that the fresh wind of the Spirit is indeed up to its transforming work in our midst. The "hunger to belong" and the necessity of communal identity has never been felt more strongly in our cultural setting. People long to be connected to a spiritual power that is beyond reason, and they are searching for relationship with others who share that same hunger. More important still, the mounting insecurities of life on this planet have us all searching for meaning to our existence that is not simply "put off" until we all get to heaven or deposited into retirement accounts until we all get to age 65.

There is the growing realization that rather than identity and even salvation being individual, both take shape in the context of community. More and more people are coming to understand that we come to faith and salvation *through* the church, *in the context of* the church, or *through interaction with* the church rather than in spite of her. Our communal worship experiences offer visions of the divine presence to the world rather than either a group of people keeping and enforcing their rules of religion or a marketing strategy offering up an exciting entertainment package.

A community of this sort cannot be created by rules or coercion or charismatic leaders. Love is not the result of coercion but is a relational response. Because we love God, we are learning to love one another. The relationship we have with him as our Heavenly Father is teaching us to regard one another as sisters and brothers. The love we have and seek to display toward Christ is transforming the way we react to one another. To think that such a community could be the result of our human plans, methods, and work is as foolish a notion as thinking we could propel a sailboat by standing on the decks and puffing at the sails with our breath. When a community of love is produced, it is the activity of God in our midst.

The church is called to bear witness to the awesome story of Creator God who is love, who came to us as the embodiment of love, who now indwells us through his Spirit and calls us to be love. The challenge is not to do random acts of kindness or to participate in occasional marriage seminars—but to *be* love to one another and to the world. The invitation to enter into the reign of God and live in loving relationship, to have our selfish desires and hateful attitudes transformed into life and world-changing service has never been more appealing than it is in our time. Young and old alike in our world are tired of division and the game called "going to church on Sunday." Any definition of "being Christian" that does not holistically—understood in terms of both *whole* and *holy*—address and embrace human existence has been weighed and found wanting. By the power of God's Spirit in us, the church as the incarnation of his love invites us into relational love not just within a localized group but in the world.

The great obstacle that has confronted God's people historically in this process is the Satanic temptation that Jesus himself
was offered in the wilderness: the offer to seize power and control for ourselves, to have
authority comparable to that
of the "kingdoms" of the
world. We think that is why
earthly models of existence
have been so alluring to
Christians. In any age, the
church has often begun to
look like the controlling
power and political structures
around it. The early church
was surrounded by empire,
and not so surprisingly took
on the status of empire as the
Holy Catholic Church when
the Roman Empire faded away. The days of feudal lords and fiefdoms were matched by churches and powerful bishops. In our
own nation, the democratic form of government with its constitutional foundations had led to democratic churches with the
New Testament as the constitution. And as business and technology created a market and consumer-driven society, churches
assumed business structures and market-driven strategies for
evangelism. When we step back and observe what has happened, we profess shock and surprise? Why? It is quite the natural process that is easily adopted as an alternative to the supernatural one God intended.

> *Thy nature, gracious Lord,
> impart;
> Come quickly from above;
> Write Thy new Name upon
> my heart,
> Thy new best Name of love.*
>
> —Charles Wesley

We should hasten to add, however, that one of the difficulties,
at least in our own time, has been the fact that several of the good
strategies that have been employed in the political and business
environments have some discernible basis in Scripture. Ideas
about community more often found in twelve-step programs than
in churches were rooted in the conceptual understandings of
community discovered in Scripture. Business management models that emphasize employee input and participatory management

strategies have their basis in Scripture as well. But when those strategies have been deployed in the world and then worked their way back to the church, they often have returned with all of the worldly power and control games that feed our worst inclinations. Compassionate service offered from self-sacrificing love winds up being replaced by religious self-promotion.

"But from the beginning it was not so"—to borrow Jesus' phrase regarding God's creation intent for male and female. If the church had acted as an incarnation of God's love rather than a corporation in which jockeying for power is the constant reality, it would have been spared most of its many episodes of division across two millennia. Very few of those rifts were because some person or group abandoned the gospel. Most of them have been competitions to see whose hands would control the levers of human power—property, money, jobs, and the like. Most had to do not with the abandonment of Scripture's authority but with the interpretation of what were sometimes obscure texts (e.g., the nature of the millennium) or even over the methodology that should be used for interpreting texts (e.g., what the "silence" of Scripture on a given subject means).

Most of these controversies have centered on strong human personalities, and thus—to use biblical language—are completely "of the flesh." Church fights tend to be rooted in jealousy and to play out in mean-spirited quarrels. If that sounds like too harsh a judgment, listen to this language from Paul: "For as long as there is jealousy and quarreling among you, are you not of the flesh, and behaving according to human inclinations?" (1 Cor. 3:3). The beautiful chapter on love at 1 Corinthians 13 is not a freestanding poem the apostle wrote so we would have readings for wedding ceremonies. It was his proposed antidote for the toxic disagreements threatening the unity of the church at Corinth.[2]

## Conclusion

Jesus came to model a life of love and service, to model the mystery of human and divine in the flesh. In his death and resurrection and exaltation, he created a vision and pathway for us to share in those same realities. Indwelled and empowered by the Spirit, we have been invited to serve one another and the world as the embodied Christ. While we live in the midst of this ongoing transformation, we will not see everything alike. But we can continue to see Jesus. Perhaps with that focus and through his lenses of love we can enact his kingdom promises, even when we faithfully and respectfully disagree about some of the details of what it means to be Jesus in our time and in our world.

By taking the call to be the living body in Christ seriously, the microcosm of the kingdom of God that we call church will constantly intermingle multiple citizenships and our wonderfully diverse personalities. We are citizens of heaven and citizens of particular nations and cultural settings on earth. The fact that this microcosm is always imbedded in the social circumstances of the humans whom God has invited into his story means that the corporate "personalities" of each microcosm will be simultaneously alike and different from each other. Our confession of Jesus as Lord will always be the same. Our particular testimony of Christ to our world will reflect each community's efforts to embody Christ for the time and circumstances in which they live. On the one hand, it is thus fairly obvious that the form of the microcosm in Papua New Guinea will not be the same as the microcosm in Iraq or the microcosm in Denver. As Paul sought to become "all things to all people" for the sake of the gospel, so communities of faith today will reflect that same sort of flexibility. Empowered by the living presence of God in us through the Holy Spirit, we will seek to be Jesus to our world in our time and location. We will seek, as a microcosm of the kingdom, to manifest God's reign both within the group and in the larger community with which it interacts.

This means, however, that identity must always be found in Christ rather than in a list of fixed and distinctive similarities and differences among franchises, branches, or tribes. This will take us out of comparison games and consumer shopping for churches and engage us instead in the "taste-and-see" process of experiencing the kingdom of God in a specific local church through the fruit of the Spirit seen and tasted from within. It is still true:

Christians are to be known by our love. It is the fruit of the Spirit flowing out of each microcosm called church that ultimately defines the once-for-all redeemed in Christ—*the church*.

## Notes

1. George Barna and Mark Hatch, *Boiling Point* (Ventura, CA: Regal Books, 2001), pp. 235-236.

2. Precisely because we do not wish to leave this discussion at the level of theory, we have attempted in an Appendix to model a relational approach to Scripture and community regarding controversial issues in our own time.

Christianity entered history as a new social order, or rather a new social dimension. From the very beginning Christianity was not primarily a "doctrine," but exactly a "community." There was not only a "Message" to be proclaimed and delivered, and "Good News" to be declared. There was precisely a New Community, distinct and peculiar, in the process of growth and formation, to which members were called and recruited. Indeed "fellowship" (koinonia) was the basic category of Christian existence.

—Georges Florovsky

# POSTSCRIPT

---

*We declare to you what was from the beginning, what
we have heard, what we have seen with our eyes, what we
have looked at and touched with our hands, concerning the
word of life—this life was revealed, and we have seen it and
testify to it, and declare to you the eternal life that was with
the Father and was revealed to us—we declare to you what
we have seen and heard so that you also may have fellowship (hoinonia) with us; and truly our fellowship (koinonia)
is with the Father and with his Son Jesus Christ. We are writing these things so that our joy may be complete.*
　　　　　　　　　　　　　　—1 John 1:1-4

Church is not an afterthought with God. The divine purpose
from eternity past has been that "through the church the
wisdom of God in its rich variety might now be made known to
the rulers and authorities in the heavenly places." And far
beyond anything we can think or dream, ask or imagine, God is
willing to work through the church to glorify Christ Jesus to all
generations. How did we lose that magnificent vision?

God took human form as Jesus of Nazareth. The very "fullness of God" dwelled in him and became visible in his personality, behaviors, and relationships. The church is called to

incarnate God's image and make it visible again for all those suc-
ceeding generations who did not see it in Jesus. When did we
relinquish that mission to the world?

Christ Jesus is the "cornerstone chosen and precious" whom
God has put at the center of all heaven's redemptive purposes.
But all who have come to him for eternal life are individual "living stones" whom God wills to build into a "spiritual house, to
be a holy priesthood, to offer spiritual sacrifices acceptable to
God through Jesus Christ." What turned us into a loose heap of
rocks as an alternative to being fitted and cemented together as
a holy structure?

The Son of God has chosen and pledged himself to a bride.
That bride is not a particular saint or chosen soul. Christ's bride
is his church—his whole and entire church, not your denomination or our local congregation. And his purpose is "to present the
church to himself in splendor, without a spot or wrinkle or anything of the kind—yes, so that she may be holy and without
blemish." So when did the bride decide to become so self-
absorbed in her endowments and wealth that she became aloof,
obnoxious, and offensive to so many?

We have claimed in *The Jesus Community* that at least part
of the answer to these questions is wrapped up in Modernity's
fascination with individualism and independence. So deep and
strong has the commitment been to personal liberty and autonomy that we have been blind to the biblical truth that God's purpose is to form the disciples of Jesus into vibrant spiritual communities. From the beginning, God has wanted humankind to
bear his image and likeness within the created order (Gen. 1:26-
28). Sin spoiled that original design, but Jesus came to restore it.
God was enfleshed in Jesus, and his death and resurrection
were intended to be the means by which all who believe in him
could be empowered for humanity's original purpose of divine
image-bearing. The church is a community of the
redeemed—humans in whom God's image is fully restored and
the Holy Spirit abides—in which Jesus seeks to reproduce his
life in collective form.

Individualism defeats God's purpose for the church. The

modern church's call for people to "accept Christ as your personal Savior" has played out as a competitive environment for newly saved individuals instead of a counter-cultural society. Evangelical Protestantism has spoken both passionately and persuasively about the need for personal (i.e., individual) salvation but failed to develop a vision for what these individuals were saved to become.

So we have created institutional churches. We have embraced the passion for external correctness of form. We have produced scholars whose task is to guide us to doctrinal correctness in all particulars. We have invested billions of dollars in buildings, vestments, and competition. The fresh life of the Holy Spirit one senses in Acts of the Apostles has been traded for the fleshly alternatives of formulas, programs, and exclusion. The Spirit of God is being held prisoner in the institutional church.

Whereas we have reduced the redeemed community of God to an institution in which we can be spared close interdependent association, part of the church's original purpose is to rescue us from such isolation. We are not meant to be protected from one another but to be in such intimate—and sometimes irritating—contact with one another that we are forced to abandon self for Jesus' sake, self-seeking for true agape (Gk, other-centered concern).

So we close by repeating the refrain of this volume: *God's strategy for winning the world is beauty.* The church—like Eve in the original purpose of God to have his glory borne by humankind—is taken out of Jesus, is designed to live as his loving companion, and is destined to be with him forever. The church is ultimately inseparable from and indispensable to Christ. As his true and loving companion who awaits his return, the church lives now as a visible community within which every member is progressively remade in community. A local church that serves as a laboratory for the gospel in human lives and relationships. A Jesus community.

When the divine purpose to incarnate the gospel in communities of discipleship becomes dominant over the present cultural model of Christianity as business, we will actually experience the righteousness Jesus brought as an alternative to that of the Pharisees and scribes. When we get our hands off the levers of power and control and yield them again to the Holy Spirit, the church as interdependence, self-denial, patience, meekness, and love will emerge. When the church allows Christ-presence to be real, tangible, and collective with us, people will say, "God is really among you!" And they will come alongside the beautiful bride, be caught up in her passion for her Savior-Groom, and be saved.

Our reclaimed understanding of the Spirit's presence and activity in our midst both energizes and serves as living reminder. We are secure in the knowledge that we have been saved; we live out our calling as those who are being saved; we await the consummation of the ages when we will be saved. When our fellowship with God is realized in a true and visible fellowship with one another, our joy will be complete! Until that day comes, we lament all that must remain unrealized in the divine will. Yet, even in lament we live in hope and we cry out, *Our Lord, come!*

# *Appendix*

As a means of suggesting how our understanding of relational faith might be lived out in a particular church, consider a couple of issues facing Christians today that illustrate the distinction between unhealthy teaching or practice that breaks relationship with God and honest differences in which community is preserved. Our two examples at first look very similar, for they relate to gender and sexuality. As it turns out, however, they are very different—homosexuality and female roles in the life of the church. These hotly debated issues are chosen not because we have definitive answers—we do not in either instance—but as illustrations of how we have attempted to address them through the lens of relational faith and contextualized conversation in our own microcosm, the Woodmont Hills church. We do not suggest that others should necessarily agree with our conclusions. Rather we are seeking to model an approach to Scripture and community life in the Spirit in faithful, responsible ways. In other settings, we ourselves might draw differing conclusions or use different particulars to illustrate the heart attitude and practice we are advocating.

## Homosexuality

Unless you have been off the planet for the past few years, you are aware that tremendous pressure continues to be put on churches to recast their historic position on homosexuality. Every time homosexuality is mentioned in either the Old or New Testament, it is condemned. Is there something about this judgment that is permanent and transcultural? Or does it simply reflect ancient taboos and the homophobic prejudice of someone such as Paul? There are plenty of biblical scholars ready to take the position that the biblical view of homosexual behavior is as antiquated and inappropriate to our time and place as some of its statements about slavery or females.

To deny that humans are sexual beings is to deny the obvious. And a failure to develop a theology of human personhood that affirms our sexual nature has been a serious failure in Christian theology. That failure, in turn, has left Christians with the undesirable options of either embracing a worldly point of view or being reactionary in most of our teaching.

> Then God said, "Let us make humankind in our image, according to our likeness; and let them have dominion over the fish of the sea, and over the birds of the air, and over the cattle, and over all the wild animals of the earth, and over every creeping thing that creeps upon the earth." So God created humankind in his image, in the image of God he created them; male and female he created them. God blessed them, and God said to them, "Be fruitful and multiply, and fill the earth and subdue it...." (Gen.1:26-28a, NRSV).

The critical thing about this text is not sex but personhood. All human beings are created to bear the image of God. That we are both male and female in our humanity is not an evolutionary accident but a divine choice. It is obvious from this first biblical text about the matter that human sexuality allows God's image-bearers to participate with him in the act of creation. From texts that follow in Scripture, it is equally plain that sex serves purposes other than the generation of new life. It is a means for drawing humans into community with one another as families, friends, and covenantal partners.

At the beginning of the human experience in Eden, God was concerned to provide Adam a "helper"—not for work but for companionship, not for sexual gratification but for deliverance from social isolation.[1] Adam had animals for amusement and work, but he was "alone" in some significant way. "I will make him a helper as his partner," said the Lord God (Gen. 2:18b, NRSV). When Eve had been created, she was brought to the man and received by him as "bone of my bones and flesh of my flesh." The story ends with these words: "Therefore a man leaves his father and his mother and clings to his wife, and they become one flesh. And the man and his wife were both naked, and were not ashamed" (Gen. 2:24-25).

As two embodied persons, Adam and Eve were to become "one flesh." This language is not to be heard as euphemistic sensitivity but as a remarkable comment on the depth of commitment between two embodied souls. The union of a man and woman in marital sex is so complete that they can be thought of as having not two but only one body. There is certainly nothing negative toward human sexual expression in these opening lines of Scripture. The nakedness (i.e., vulnerability) of the man and woman to each other in their sexual natures was hardly a source of shame. It was joyous and celebratory—as that of the lover and his beloved in Song of Solomon.

Homosexuality is wrong because it negates the procreative design of human sexuality. It seeks to satisfy the innate desire for bonding within love through a means other than the one God established in the created order. Thus homosexuality is wrong not because it violates a command but because it violates the divine will as expressed in creation itself. It is the unholy violation of the created order that generates the biblical prohibitions. These proscriptions are thus universal and transcultural, not rooted in a particular time, place, or prejudice. They are rooted in the narrative of God's nature and activity as related in Scripture; they cannot be abandoned without simultaneously embracing the notion that Scripture is no longer authoritative for Christianity.

Homosexuality is unlike racism, slavery, or female roles in the life of the church for the simple reason that only one of these issues is rooted in creation itself. All the others have to do with the use and abuse of power in the human community. Even so, we must be careful against being understood to endorse for a moment some of the hateful attitudes that some believers exhibit toward homosexuals. To the contrary, this is one of those opportunities in our culture for the church to be the incarnation of love to persons whose behavior we cannot sanction.

We, the church, have the opportunity to demonstrate, in our words and in our lives, God's love for the homosexual person. If we truly love, we will act on that love. We must start by eradicating our negative responses to homosexual people. Stop the queer jokes and insults; they hurt others. We must deal with our own emotional reactions; we must decide to love. We must repudiate violence and intolerance toward persons of homosexual orientation. We must change the church so that it is a place where those who feel homosexual desire can be welcomed. The church must become a sanctuary where repentant men and women can share with others the sexual desires they feel and still receive prayerful support and acceptance...

Now the second part of our call—to speak the truth. If we truly love, we will not shrink from speaking God's view of homosexual behavior. Do not be deceived: increasingly today we are defined as unloving solely for viewing homosexuality as immoral, regardless of the compassion we exhibit. Nevertheless, we must strive to be loving when we voice our opposition. Compassion in no way entails an acceptance of the gay lifestyle any more than it entails affirming an adulterer's infidelity.[2]

The challenge to conservative churches is less to join our voices in confessing that we regard Scripture as God-breathed communication than to eat with, pray with, and otherwise encourage persons who feel homosexual or lesbian desire. Where do such feelings originate? Are there genetic factors that predispose certain people to these yearnings?[3] We don't presume to be wise enough to answer all the questions we can raise about this issue—much less those offered by so many others. What we are forced to confess by our understanding of the gospel is that all saved persons are not only forgiven of the guilt of their past but promised empowerment from the Holy Spirit to live as children of God, to put off an old way of life, and to embrace one that is increasingly renewed in holiness (Col. 3:5ff; cf. 2 Cor. 5:17). Jesus was willing to be criticized by the champions of orthodoxy for associating with those whose sins had made them outcasts (Luke 15:1-2); perhaps the time will yet come when his followers will be less concerned about our image before critics than the welfare of anyone who is struggling to find God. From our perspective, more is at stake here than a decision by Christ's followers to associate with persons who have broken a rule about sexual conduct. It is about seeing people through the eyes of Jesus—seeing persons rather than issues, focusing on their likeness to God rather than on preserving our institutional reputation.

## Female Roles in Church Life

For the last three decades at least, churches have been wrestling with the issue of female roles in the life of the church. More specifically still, we have been trying to figure out what it means for male and female to have a single identity in Christ. Like our surrounding culture, the language of "all humans being created equal" rarely has been matched by actual classless treatment of others. As the United States has struggled in spurts and stops to treat men and women with fairness—whether the particular concern was voting rights or equal pay for equal work—churches have struggled to understand the visible roles of women in our worship assemblies.

The sad truth is that in many cases a good argument can be made that the church has been a slow but steady follower of culture, rather than being the shaping influence for good in culture. It could be argued that it became acceptable for women to stop wearing hats to church only after it became unfashionable in popular culture. Some insist it became acceptable for men to wear longer hair at church only after it became a cultural norm. And many would suggest that in our own time church is still simply following culture when we allow women to take active participatory roles in our worship assemblies.

We suggest that the real issue is not, nor has it been in the past, simply a matter of culture leading the church. Nor is the real issue a matter of some people taking the Bible seriously and others just ignoring Scripture for the sake of contemporary appeal. Those advocating more active roles for women in our worship assemblies take the Bible just as seriously as those who believe women should be "silent" in those assemblies. The question for all of us is not what the Bible says, but how and why. If *what* were our only concern, we could read it straightforwardly as God's rule book for human behavior apart from any and all cultural contexts. But common sense already showed us that the "holy kiss" and washing feet were culturally conditioned statements. Unlike the issue with homosexuality, there is certainly nothing about lips touching cheeks or water being applied to feet that intrinsically challenges the work of God in the created order. So we were appropriately led to expect that these commands might be conditioned by culture. Neither is there anything that challenges the divine order in creation by having women partner with males in serving God. So isn't it at least possible that there could be cultural conditioning at work in some of the statements about how men and women function in the life of the church? And couldn't Christians disagree in good faith about the interpretation of those statements without any party to the discussion jettisoning a high view of Scripture as the Word of God?

Remember, our fundamental conviction is that the Bible is the story of God, a dramatic narrative that announces and reveals and invites us into participation and relationship with God and one another. Every scene in that story has been set in some historical human context. Those cultural settings always have been changing and changeable. In the first century, the community of faith—the body of Christ—was, to use Paul's phrase to the Philippians, "working out their salvation" as God himself was working and willing his good pleasure through them (Phil. 2:12-13).

We find ourselves engaged in the same divine-human effort—only our cultural circumstances are clearly not the same as those of the first-century world. Male and female relationships in the Hellenistic world of Paul's experience have both similarities to and differences from our time and place. The question is, how do we hear the texts—specifically the words written by Paul to the Corinthians and his words written to Timothy and to the church in Ephesus? Do we assume Paul is issuing unilateral rules that have no specific relationship to the cultural setting of people in Corinth and Ephesus? Or do we read these texts and hear Paul trying to insure that the people of Corinth and Ephesus are not prevented from seeing Jesus because males and females in the church are behaving in bizarre ways? And if indeed the latter is true (i.e., that these texts were intended to illustrate how first-century Christians should behave in ways that would not compromise their witness to the world), what happens today when in our more egalitarian context our worship assemblies are experienced as male-only events?

Even more to the point, perhaps, are those events in our assemblies for which we have no written protocol but to which we have assigned "male-only" roles in the name of God-given authority that prohibits female participation. Most notable in that category is the serving of bread and cup trays in what became the traditional manner, at least in the last century. Designated men stood and walked through the aisles, passing the trays from row to row. We are hard-pressed to name when such service became an issue of "authority over" others, but we have experienced the tremendous angst that follows any suggestion that women be allowed to stand in the aisle and serve. Why? Are the bread and cup somehow authenticated by male servers? Is it a kind of slippery-slope fear that says "If they serve communion today, they will preach or become shepherd-overseers tomorrow"? And just how great should the fear be that some communities might allow even that to happen? Will Jesus Christ no longer be Savior and Lord? Will this be a doctrinal heresy that denies the existence of God or his call to holy living? Will this be a denial of Scripture as heaven's authoritative word? Again, in what sense does Scripture come to us as an authoritative word? As the rules? As the narrative invitation of God to live in community with him? What does it mean to live in creation-design relationship with him and at the same time live in Christ where there is neither Jew or Gentile, slave or free, male or female?

## Conclusion

Perhaps the real question is this: How can humans made in the image of God, and now re-created in Christ to be fully human and divine, live out that calling in loving ways? For at the heart of our humanity is the intellectual and emotional ability to think and choose and decide—and not be clones. At the heart of our human identity in Christ is also innate difference, all the things that are not equal about us. As in-Christ-ones, we are called to see ourselves and one another with new creation understandings that restore God's paradise intent for relationship—with him and with each other. To claim the language of Paul, "And all of us, with unveiled faces, seeing the glory of the Lord as though reflected in a mirror, are being transformed into the same image from one degree of glory to another; for this comes from the Lord, the Spirit" (2 Cor. 3:18).

*Notes*

1. See Deut. 33:7 and Psa. 33:20 where forms of the word translated "helper" refer to divine deliverance.

2. Stanton L. Jones, "The Loving Opposition," *Christianity Today* (19 July 1993): 19-25; as reprinted in David K. Clark and Robert V. Rakestraw, *Readings in Christian Ethics—Vol. 2: Issues and Applications* (Grand Rapids: Baker Books, 1996), p. 210.

3. See the work by Stanton L. Jones and Mark A. Yarhouse, *Homosexuality: The Use of Scientific Research in the Church's Moral Debate* (Downers Grove, IL: Inter-Varsity Press, 2000).